BUILDING SUSTAINABLE HEALTHCARE SOCIAL ENTERPRISES IN INDIA

An innovative Business Model with the Islamic concept of Cash Waqf

DR. MOHAMMED ASLAM KHAN

STARDOM BOOKS

www.StardomBooks.com

STARDOM BOOKS
112 Bordeaux Ct.
Coppel, TX 75019, USA

Copyright © 2023 by Dr. Mohammed Aslam Khan

All rights reserved. No part of this book may be reproduced or used in any manner without written permission of the copyright owner except for the use of quotations in a book review.

FIRST EDITION OCTOBER 2023

STARDOM BOOKS, LLC.
112 Bordeaux Ct. Coppel, TX 75019, USA

www.stardombooks.com

Stardom Books, United States
Stardom Alliance, India

The author and publishers have made all reasonable efforts to contact copyright holders for permission and apologize for any omissions or errors in the form of credits given. Corrections may be made to future editions.

BUILDING SUSTAINABLE HEALTHCARE SOCIAL ENTERPRISES IN INDIA

Dr. Mohammed Aslam Khan

p. 146
cm. 13.5 X 21.5

Category:
Business and Economics/Entrepreneurship

ISBN: 978-1-957456-30-0

DEDICATION

I humbly dedicate this book to my dear father, a remarkable man of resilience and determination.

This book is a tribute to my father, who never had the opportunity to attend school but toiled vigorously as a daily wage laborer, rickshaw puller, and shepherd in the villages of Uttar Pradesh. In 1964, he embarked on a courageous journey to Mumbai, where he found himself navigating the challenging path of a laborer, working tirelessly in coal, scrap, and fruit shops. Eventually, he became a hawker, selling and delivering loaves of bread in the towering buildings of South Mumbai, facing the challenges imposed on hawkers who were not allowed to use elevators.

With an unwavering vision to secure a brighter future for his children, he boldly decided to relocate them from the village of Uttar Pradesh to the suburbs of Mumbai. Over there, he embraced the world of metal scrap trading, diligently working to provide for his family of nine members, all within the confined walls of a humble hutment measuring a mere 9 ft x 9 ft. Against all odds, he admitted his son to the Bombay Municipal Corporation Urdu medium school and later to the MH Saboo Siddik Technical High School.

Little did he know that this pivotal decision would become the turning point in his son's life, propelling him towards academic excellence and a future filled with remarkable achievements. His son completed his engineering degree, embarked on an enriching experience in Japan and the USA for a decade, and eventually returned to India with a burning entrepreneurial spirit. In the years that followed, he established successful business ventures in the realms of information technology and healthcare, leaving an indelible mark as the pioneer of India's first-ever fully Shariah-compliant listed company at the Bombay Stock Exchange. The foundation laid by my father's unwavering determination and commitment to education paved the way for a remarkable journey of success.

This dedication is a testament to my father's sacrifices and the unyielding love and determination he poured into his son's education. It is an acknowledgment of his extraordinary efforts to break the cycle of poverty and create opportunities where none seemed possible. My father's resilience and firm belief in the power of education has inspired me beyond measure.

To my father, a beacon of strength and a true role model, this book is dedicated to you. Your sacrifices, perseverance, and unwavering support have paved the way for my achievements, and I am forever grateful for your indomitable spirit.

CONTENTS

	ACKNOWLEDGEMENTS	i
	FOREWORD	v
1	INTRODUCTION	1
2	CURRENT HEALTHCARE SYSTEM AND ITS LOOPHOLES	7
3	HEALTH FINANCING IN INDIA	15
4	THE DIFFERENT SOCIAL ENDOWMENT MODELS	23
5	EVERYTHING ABOUT SOCIAL ENTERPRISE	31
6	THE JOURNEY TO EXPLORE THE EFFECTIVENESS OF ENDOWMENT IN HEALTHCARE	47
7	THE SUSTAINIBILITY OF THE BUSINESS MODEL	63
8	THE IMPLEMENTATION OF THE SUSTAINABLE BUSINESS MODEL IN THE SOCIAL ENTERPRISE	81
9	SUSTAINABLE SOCIAL ENTERPRISE WITH CASH WAQF INVESTMENT	95
10	CONCLUSION	115
	BIBLIOGRAPHY	125
	ABOUT THE AUTHOR	131

ACKNOWLEDGMENTS

Before anything else, I would like to pledge my devotion to God, the most merciful & the most gracious.

I begin this acknowledgment by offering my heartfelt praise and gratitude to the Almighty Allah for his blessings, guidance, and endless mercy throughout the journey of completing my book titled *"Building Sustainable Healthcare Social Enterprises in India: An Innovative Business Model with the Islamic Concept of Cash Waqf."* His grace and benevolence have persuaded me to embark on this meaningful endeavor.

I express my deepest gratitude to all my teachers, from the earliest years of my education to the esteemed individuals who have guided me at various stages of my academic and professional journey. Your knowledge, wisdom, and dedication have shaped my intellect and fostered a love for learning that pushes me to create a better version of myself every day and move ahead. I am indebted to your tireless efforts and commitment to imparting knowledge.

First and foremost, I would like to thank Mufti Abdul Qadir Barkatulla, Judge, Islamic Sharia Council, London, for being the source of inspiration behind the writing of this book. His belief in the significance of sharing knowledge has been a powerful inspiration, motivating me to diligently document and disseminate the insights gained throughout this endeavor. His visionary thinking and challenge to explore equity capital funding through the Islamic concept of cash waqf have shaped the innovative business model discussed in this book. I sincerely express my gratitude to Mufti Abdul Qadir Barkatullah for his exceptional contributions, unwavering guidance, and profound inspiration throughout the entire journey of developing the business model and authoring this book. His visionary outlook and steadfast commitment to Islamic economics and finance have played an indispensable role in shaping the ideas meticulously presented within these pages.

I extend my heartfelt appreciation to my supervisors during my postdoctoral research project at the Markfield Institute of Higher Education, Leicestershire, UK. The guidance, expertise, and mentorship of Dr. Faizal Ahmad Manjoo and Dr. Zahid Parvez have been invaluable in shaping my action research and refining my idea of developing a social enterprise based on the Islamic concept of cash waqf investment to provide affordable healthcare services in

India. Your immense knowledge, critical insights, and dedication to academic rigor have played a pivotal role in shaping the structure and content of this book. Your mentorship has genuinely been an honor and a privilege.

I am immensely grateful to Prof. Dr. Irena Markova from the University of Finance, Business, and Entrepreneurship, Sofia, partner institution of the University of Sheffield, UK, for her guidance and supervision during my doctoral dissertation. Your commitment to academic excellence and unwavering support has been instrumental in my growth as an action researcher and writer.

I would like to extend my heartfelt appreciation to Mr. Alan Ross for his invaluable contribution in helping me build my action research skills during my Masters in Research program at Lancaster University, UK. His guidance, expertise, and unconditional support have been foundational in shaping my applied research capabilities and have greatly influenced the content and methodology of this book.

I am immensely thankful to Dr. Shariq Nisar, a well-known figure in the Indian financial sector and Director at Rizvi Institute of Management Studies and Research, and Mufti Mohammed Ashfaq Kazi, Chief Mufti of Juma Masjid Mumbai and esteemed Shariah Advisor, for their invaluable contributions to this book. Your knowledgeable advice, in-depth understanding of Islamic finance principles, and insights into the concept of cash waqf have enriched the discussions and provided a strong base for the innovative business model presented herein. I extend special gratitude to Dr. Shariq Nisar for his meticulous review of the entire book, which significantly improved its quality and coherence.

I extend my sincere appreciaton to Mr. Nazim Sawant and Mr. Yusuf Shaikh of Saksham Social Venture, an initiative of GoBizLAB – Center for Innovation & Entrepreneurship, for their collaboration, support, and sharing their practical experiences in the field of healthcare social enterprises in India. Your real-world perspectives and expertise have added depth and authenticity to the concepts explored in this book.

I am grateful to my business partners at Octaware Technologies Limited, including Mr. Shahnawaz Shaikh, Mr. Siraj Gunwan, Mr. Merajuddin Shaikh, and Mr. Anwer Baghdadi. Your insights, expertise, and collaborative spirit have enhanced the business strategies discussed in this book, making them more robust and practical.

I am indebted to my business colleagues at Transpact Enterprises Limited, Dr. Anis Choudhary and Mr. Sudhir Bania. Your support, collaboration, and dedication to technological innovation have been pivotal in developing sustainable solutions for healthcare social enterprises.

I am thankful to my colleagues at RIDA Foundation, including Mr. Naseem Shah, Dr. Parvez Khan, Dr. Ravi Varma, Mr. Samir Shaikh, and Dr. Noor-ul- Hasan, for their collaboration, valuable input, and shared commitment to making a positive social impact. Your expertise and dedication to societal well-being have inspired and influenced the ideas presented in this book.

I am grateful to the publishing team and would like to thank Mr. Raam Anand, Ranjitha Vijaykumar, and Rekha Krishnaprasad for their support and guidance throughout the publication process. Your professionalism and commitment to excellence have contributed to the quality of this book. Additionally, I express my appreciation to Sthitodhi Das for her meticulous efforts in refining the content and ensuring its clarity and coherence.

Lastly, I am immensely thankful to all the individuals, organizations, and institutions whose research, publications, and initiatives in the field of sustainable healthcare social enterprises have indirectly contributed to this book. Your collective efforts have paved the way for this work and have inspired me to contribute to the betterment of society through innovative solutions.

In conclusion, I offer my heartfelt gratitude to God Almighty for his blessings, my dear parents for their endless support, and all my teachers for their guidance and knowledge. I am deeply thankful for the firm belief and encouragement of my wife and children, who have been a constant source of strength. To all the individuals and organizations mentioned above, your contributions have been invaluable, and I am immensely grateful for your support and collaboration.

Dr. Mohammed Aslam Khan.

FOREWORD

In this insightful book, **"Building Sustainable Healthcare Social Enterprises in India: An Innovative Business Model with the Islamic Concept of Cash Waqf,"** we are introduced to the unique challenges and opportunities faced by India in the domain of healthcare. The COVID-19 crisis has tremendously challenged the healthcare system while amplifying the struggle for financial sustainability experienced by social enterprises. However, amidst these challenges, many new opportunities emerged. Among them is the Government of India initiative to introduce social enterprises exchange for systematic raising the human capital and services stock. Their proposal in July 2019 to establish a social stock exchange aimed at helping social enterprises raise funds through equity listing was a significant step forward. Moreover, in December 2022, the Bombay Stock Exchange (BSE) and National Stock Exchange (NSE) launched the Social Stock Exchange, providing a platform for social enterprises to raise capital by attracting social investors.

This timely and transformative guide comes after 2014's Corporate Social Responsibility (CSR) obligations enacted to the high-end corporate sector. It is at a crucial moment as the author explores the role of cash waqf in funding the social enterprise business model. By delving into this subject, the book offers valuable insights and guidance that will empower social entrepreneurs to raise funds through a new and unique model of cash waqf (liquid endowment) investment. This exploration of cash waqf serves as an innovative solution to financial sustainability. It highlights its significance as an alternate source of interest-free and highly gratifying financing, providing an opportunity to support and uplift humanity. Furthermore, by engaging in cash waqf, individuals can have the opportunity to earn eternal rewards in the hereafter, making it a truly noble endeavor.

Through a comprehensive understanding of India's healthcare system and the financing landscape, this book introduces the Sustainable Social Enterprise Business Model (SSEBM) supported by cash waqf investment. Drawing upon the author's postdoctoral research and experience as a social entrepreneur in the healthcare sector, the book emphasizes every individual's fundamental right to healthcare, regardless of social hierarchies. It offers practical guidance by exploring various funding methods and social endowment models, catering to the needs of social entrepreneurs and social investors. Theoretical and empirical contributions make this work an essential resource for academicians and researchers in the field of social enterprise, financial sustainability, and business models. The conceptual framework, theoretical model, and empirical findings provide valuable insights into the pathways from social investment to the financial sustainability of social enterprises.

By bridging the gap between academic literature and practical sustainability, this book serves as a blueprint for extending the SSEBM model to various sectors, fostering a holistic understanding of social enterprise. With a revolutionary perspective on healthcare services and the integration of finance and healthcare, **"Building Sustainable Healthcare Social Enterprises in India: An Innovative Business Model with the Islamic Concept of Cash Waqf"** brings forth a paradigm shift in social entrepreneurship, investment strategies, and academic research in this sector. The author's passion and dedication shine through, making this book an indispensable guide for social investors, social entrepreneurs, and scholars seeking to make a sustainable societal impact.

Let us embark on this transformative journey together, embracing the revolution and redefining our approach to healthcare, social enterprise, and academic research. Through collective efforts, we can create a future where accessible and affordable healthcare becomes a reality for all.

Mufti Abdul Kadir Barkatulla.

INTRODUCTION

As one of the most populous countries in the world, India faces both unique challenges and unprecedented opportunities in the sphere of healthcare. According to the World Health Organization, healthcare embraces all the goods and efficient services designed to promote health, including "preventive, curative and palliative interventions, whether directed to individuals or to populations." The delivery of healthcare is a significant problem for India and other developing countries due to out-of-pocket expenditure by consumers as the primary source of financing healthcare. Thus, there has been increasing concern over the affordable healthcare delivery system in India over the past two decades due to low health financing. In recent years, social enterprise as an alternative method of delivering affordable healthcare has attracted a lot of attention.

As you skim through the pages, you will gain impactful insights on the status of healthcare in India, shariah-based endowment (waqf) & cash-waqf based models that help in funding, and how social enterprises are crucial in delivering affordable healthcare. In Islam, the concept of "waqf" has been widely aligned with the spirit of charity endorsed by the holy Quran. It implies the endowment of property to Allah, under the premise that the transfer will benefit the needy and underprivileged people.

The idea of a social enterprise was developed in the U.K. in 1970 to counter the traditional commercial enterprise.[1] Social enterprises have a social mission to fulfill. Many practitioners and researchers have proposed expanding the uses of the endowment to help social enterprises achieve their social mission. Social enterprises have been proven to be a potentially innovative and sustainable solution to accessible and affordable healthcare services in India.[2] Financial sustainability is considered to be a prerequisite for successful social investment decision-making and social enterprise success. The financial sustainability of social enterprises is a holistic concept that involves sustainable social enterprise and a business model. However, social enterprises might fail to secure social investment leading to financial sustainability and a complex issue for many social enterprises. While extensive research about financial sustainability has a long history in the sustainable social enterprise and business model disciplines, a number of important challenges remain unresolved till date. For instance, academic research in the sustainable social enterprise and business model disciplines today lacks sufficient insight to answer how social investment in equity capital funding leads to the financial sustainability of the social enterprise. Moving ahead, the social enterprise and shariah-based endowment investment disciplines lack theoretical understanding of how social investment in equity capital funding could be considered cash waqf and are equally unable to develop a sustainable social enterprise business model based on the Islamic concept of cash waqf investment.

This book developed through postdoctoral research aims to address these gaps in knowledge. Positioned in the sustainable social enterprise and business model disciplines, the research provides the conceptual and theoretical underpinnings to explore the financial sustainability of the social enterprise. The inductive approach of the qualitative study is used for this research to create a conceptual framework based on the identified knowledge gap found during the literature review. It adopted an action research approach to empirically develop and test the conceptual framework of the sustainable social enterprise business model for the financial sustainability of the social enterprise. The interpretative phenomenological analysis employed semi-structured interviews of social investors to explore financial sustainability from the perspective of social investors and their investment decision-making process.

Collectively, the conceptual framework and action research study provides three distinct contributions to the sustainable social enterprise and business model literature. Firstly, the conceptual inquiry provides an important contribution in the form of a novel conceptual framework for a sustainable social enterprise business model. Secondly, a theoretical contribution is made, which includes a theoretical model and four propositions that explain pathways from social investment to financial sustainability of the social enterprise in delivering affordable healthcare services to underprivileged and needy patients at the bottom of the economic pyramid. Thirdly, an empirical contribution to the social enterprise literature is made by developing a sustainable social enterprise business model in practice and highlighting evidence regarding the social mission and financial sustainability related to social enterprise.

Since the author is a social entrepreneur in the healthcare sector, he wanted to draw light on how healthcare is the fundamental right of all human beings and how everyone should have access to it. Albeit the healthcare sector has endless shortcomings, the author introduces several ways in which healthcare can be funded for everyone irrespective of social hierarchies. This book is designed as a monograph, in which a complete and detailed description of the research performance is presented and structured into eight chapters. The flow of chapters is organized and based on the research framework.

Chapter One emphasizes on the current healthcare system and its drawbacks— It discusses the principles of healthcare, the risk factors leading to a negative impact in the present healthcare infrastructure, and the two spectrums of healthcare in India.

Chapter Two focuses on the major problems in the healthcare sector, methods to fund, and the various types of frameworks to analyze healthcare in India.

Chapter Three introduces the various kinds of social endowment models and how they help in implementing a better healthcare system.

Chapter Four covers the concept of social enterprises— the different types of social enterprises, their respective roles and funding sources in the healthcare sector, and most importantly, the concept of a business model.

Chapter Five embarks on a journey to explore the effectiveness of endowment in healthcare. It reveals the motivation behind the research, research philosophy, and design. Through an analysis of the literature, the context of various researchers' perspectives is examined and concluded by pinpointing at the main observations, inconsistencies, and gaps in the field of study relating to the scope of this research. In addition, the chapter discusses the main reasons for choosing the action research method and the advantages and disadvantages of the chosen method and highlights the data analysis tools and ethical considerations of the work.

Chapter Six discusses the sustainability of the business model and argues why social enterprises are worthy of investigation. It outlines theoretical-methodological aspects of introducing a social enterprise with shariah-based endowment investment. It describes the conceptual framework of stages in the development of the healthcare business model of social enterprise with the shariah-based endowment investment.

Chapter Seven provides the practical aspects to the implementation of a healthcare business model of social enterprise. It describes the overall action research cycles consisting of iterative cycles in an attempt to develop and test a new healthcare business model of a social enterprise with shariah-based endowment investment. Moreover, the research interviews, the research informants' profiles, and the data collected are demonstrated in this chapter.

Chapter Eight reports the results of the study that are directed by the research questions and discusses the findings of semi-structured interviews and results of the empirical investigations and builds a theoretical model.

Finally, the Conclusion summarizes the theoretical and practical contributions along with the limitations of the research. It also provides suggestions for future research.

1

CURRENT HEALTHCARE SYSTEM AND ITS LOOPHOLES

India is an abode to one of the world's largest healthcare systems. According to the International Trade Administration (2022), healthcare has become one of our country's largest sectors, both in terms of revenue and employment. The public healthcare sector encompasses 18% of total outpatient care and 44% of total inpatient care. As the second most populous country in the world, India has faced several hindrances in uplifting its healthcare sector. However, regardless of facing humongous challenges, India provides basic healthcare services to over one billion people. The paradigm of healthcare delivery is dynamic in India and other developing countries. The National Health Policy of India (NHP) recommendations in the past had prescribed for a government funded, three-tiered public health system to deliver curative healthcare services for the well-being of the common masses. In general, India has a mixed healthcare system, which is inclusive of public and private healthcare assistance contributors. The government comprises limited secondary care institutions and enhances on supplying basic healthcare services in rural areas. The healthcare services to people are provided by the government through hospitals, dispensaries, health centers and clinics. The Ministry of Health and Family Welfare at the state level has the responsibility of delivering primary healthcare services including maternal and child health services. Primary health care is offered in public hospitals by central and state governments in the urban area with no cost known as Urban Health Centre, and in the rural areas with the name Primary Health Care (PHC). In contrast to this, the private sector focuses on secondary and tertiary care institutions mostly in metropolitan areas.

Assessment of the Healthcare System

The Indian healthcare sector is growing at a rapid pace due to its strengthening coverage, services, and increasing expenditure by public and private players. The basic principles of healthcare are— Active participation of all segments of the population in strengthening and preserving the health of the population, responsibility of society and the state for the protection and promotion of public health, training of medical personnel, creating a common health system, ensuring the preservation and strengthening of public health, conservation and development of professional direction in health care etc.[1] The main functions of healthcare are— provision of health services, providing the necessary material and human resources, financial services to pay for health services, ensuring the activities of the various healthcare actors in strategic areas. According to the World Health Organization (WHO), modern health systems must achieve the following basic goals— improve the health of the nation, increase the adequacy of the healthcare system to patients, ensure fairness in the distribution of financial burden among participants in the health system.

However, the healthcare system of India lacks provision, utilization, and attainment. There are numerous distributions of services, power, and resources that have created a lack of equality in healthcare services. Moreover, rural areas in India have an inadequacy of medical professionals. Mortality threats before the age of five are higher for children living in rural areas than that of the ones living in urban metropolitan cities.[2] Despite being an overpopulated country, India has the maximum private healthcare in the world. Both medical and non-medical out-of-pocket payments often affect access to healthcare. There is a huge gap between outreach, finance and accessibility in India. In terms of non-medical costs, underprivileged people often refrain from visiting health centers due to the distance. Hence, outreach programs are mandatory for the marginalized classes of people. In contrast to medical costs, out-of-pocket hospitalization fees foreshadow access to healthcare. Without financial independence, the isolated groups cannot have the path to approach healthcare.

Risk Factors with a Negative Impact on Healthcare

The healthcare infrastructure is overburdened due to increasing population causing a challenge for the health system which includes the epidemiological shift, demographic transition and environmental changes. The issues with maternal and child mortality, HIV/AIDS and other communicable diseases created immense strain on the health system of India. The reason for health inequalities rests in the social, monetary, and political systems that lead to social stratification as per income, education, occupation, gender and race or ethnicity. The presence of these social determinants of health has been recognized as the drawbacks of the effective health system of India. The main risk factors that have a negative impact on the functioning of the healthcare system in India and necessitate its reform are:

Firstly, the division of rural and urban populations into strands. There are huge gaps between the rural and urban populations in the healthcare system which is causing the inequities in the healthcare delivery system. Approximately 64% of the population in India still lives in rural areas and has limited access to primary health care and hospitals hence, the rural population relies on alternate healthcare and government schemes. One such government scheme is the National Urban Health Mission which pays individuals for healthcare premiums, in partnership with various local private partners, which have proven ineffective to date. It is found that the effect of out-of-pocket expenditure in India is more in the rural areas than in urban areas.

Secondly, the existence of unhealthy living conditions. Poor sanitation and safe drinking water are critical determinants of effectiveness of the health system in India. More than 122 million households have no toilets and 33% lack access to latrines, over 50%

of the population (638 million) defecates in the open. Even though 211 million people gained access to improved sanitation from 1990–2008, only 31% used them. 11% of the Indian rural families dispose of child stools safely whereas 80% of the population leave their stools in the open or throw them into the garbage. Open air defecation leads to the spreading of diseases and malnutrition through parasitic and bacterial infections.

Thirdly, the need for an effective payment system. In addition to the rural-urban sectoral concern, another key factor in India's healthcare system is high out-of-pocket expenditure. 70% of the house-holds in India are facing out-of-pocket healthcare spending with no payment arrangements. The Indian government plays an important role in the healthcare system and runs several healthcare programs for those who are living at subsistence levels. All these schemes are regulated and controlled by the government of India and designed for people to pay upfront cash and then get reimbursed by filing a claim. Lack of an appropriate payment system and absence of well-established linkages between healthcare system and payment is a limitation of the health system in India.

Fourthly, the rapidly aging population. In India, aging is exponentially growing owing to the notable expansions that society has made in terms of increased life expectancy. The demand for holistic care tends to increase with the increase in the elderly population. The elderly population is expected to be 840 million in the developing countries by 2025. The Indian population of age 60 and older is expected to rise from 91.6 million, 7.5% of the total population in 2010 to 158.7 million, 11.1% of the population in 2025. The aging population puts an increased burden on the resources of the country and is an unavoidable risk factor in the health system of India.

Lastly, the manifestation of risks related to environmental degradation. Such risks can be environmental risks, both natural and man-made. The consequences of these risks are related to irreversible damage to life, health and working capacity of the population and irreparable damage to the environment. At the beginning of the 21st century there has been an increase in the magnitude of the consequences that occur every year as a result of accidents and natural disasters. There is a classification in the literature that lists 15 of the worst technogenic environmental disasters in the world as a result of human actions and mistakes in the 20th and 21st centuries.

India is one of the countries with the largest technogenic environmental disaster in the world as a result of the Bhopal disaster (December 2, 1984). The leak of toxic isocyanate methyl from Union Carbide pesticide plant in Bhopal has been recognized as the epicenter of one of the most devastating man-made disasters in history. 27 tonnes of toxic gas were released at night, with 90,000 people living. People were awakened by coughing and suffocation. 23 000 people perished. The problem of preventing and eliminating emergencies and crises should be a priority for each country. In order to overcome and minimize the adverse effects of the operation of hazardous industries, effective risk management should be conducted. The continuous changes in the internal and external environment where the industrial entities function require the application of adequate risk management. The analysis and control over the environmental risk factors are a prerequisite for effective risk management of enterprises.

The Provision of Healthcare Services in India

The healthcare services in India are divided into two spectrums— public sector and private sector. Public healthcare is generally free of cost for people below the poverty line. Originally, it was established to deliver access to healthcare benefits irrespective of class or socioeconomic status. However, it has been observed that middle-class and upper-class people with sustainable standards of living often consume public healthcare way more than people who belong to the below poverty line. With assistance from government subsidies, private health sectors infiltrated into the market in the 1980's. The private sector encompasses around 58% of the hospitals, 29% of beds, and 81% of doctors in hospitals. In India, there are three major ways healthcare can be funded— (a) Government financing (b) Health insurance (c) Private funding by consumers. Around 3.3% of GDP is spent on healthcare, out of which 41.4% is funded by the government. A slight percentage of 7 directly goes into health insurance while the rest of the 47.1% is out of pocket expenditure.

The latest estimates based on national accounts statistics indicate that private expenditure on healthcare in India is about Rs. 3,84,055 crores. Public expenditure on healthcare is about Rs. 1,85,647 crores on top of this (Table 1). Together, this sums up to 3.3 percent of GDP, with out-of-pocket expenses resulting in 52% of the share in the total health expenditure. It is also noted that even these minor public expenditures are skewed towards the wealthier communities, especially those residing in urban regions. The 90% of the users paying from the out of pocket belong to the poorest section of the society. The National data also discloses that 50 percent of the bottom of the pyramid (BOP) patients sold assets or took loans to access healthcare. Therefore, debt and asset sales are estimated to contribute significantly to financing healthcare.

Table 1. Financing Healthcare in India

	Rs. Crores	%
Public Sector	1,85,647	31.28
Social Insurance	23,957	4.04
Private Sector	3,84,055	64.68
Private Insurance	75,328	12.68
Out of Pocket	3,08,727	52
Total	**5,93,659**	**100**

(Source: National Health Accounts, 2019-20)

Public healthcare financing comes mainly from the public budgets of the state government (about 61%) and the Union government contributes 36% and local government balance of 3%. Of the total public health budget, approximately 5.1% is externally funded. Private financing is mostly out of pocket expense, mainly for hospitalization coming from savings, loans, and the sale of assets. Hence, there is a major concern regarding healthcare in India due to low health financing.

Role of CSR in Indian Healthcare

The healthcare system consists of organizations and institutions that operate to enhance, retain or recover health. In addition to the central and state government's initiative, most of the solutions for accessible and affordable healthcare problems are expected from the non-governmental organizations (NGOs) and corporate social responsibility (CSR) of private firms. Hospitals run by NGOs are heterogeneous and differ in terms of property, funding, and expenses. In the latest past, in approximately ten health-oriented projects of the Ministry of Health and Family Welfare, Government of India, NGOs have actively participated in the funding agency as health service suppliers depending on their capability level. For instance, the responsibility for offering community-based health facilities in a district covering 40 villages with a population size of 35000 has been allocated to SEWA-Rural in Gujarat. Besides healthcare facilities, NGOs also participate in several operations in preventive care, perhaps more than curative care. Several NGOs are engaged in tribal health awareness through multiple community-based methods, including door-to-door information flow, street performance, visuals, and tribal area discussions.

In India, CSR funding is compulsory for a few corporations, but initiatives for social activities are also taken by other companies. Corporates have separate departments to look after CSR activities. Health camps, eye check-up camps are the health care organizations most frequently referred to as CSR operations. The new avenues for CSR operations in the healthcare segment are women empowerment programs, emergency numbers during cardiac arrest, geriatric care, and free consultation for senior citizens. However, the healthcare initiatives undertaken by the NGOs and corporate entities under their corporate social responsibility have achieved limited success in terms of bridging the socio-economic gap as well as generating the desired level of social impact for affordable healthcare.

Along with the initiatives taken by NGOs and CSR, the Socially Responsible Investing (SRI) forum serves as a linkage between existing mass social trends and the financial performance of corporations. It tends to target industries that find it difficult to attract other types of private investment, such as healthcare, renewable energy, and rural development. Increasing numbers of service providers – such as community organizations, charities or non-profit organizations, social enterprises, social businesses, and socially impact-driven enterprises– are specialized in addressing social needs. SRI plays a critical role in preparing economies to promote the development and expand these models to benefit the poor and disadvantaged in the healthcare segment.

India is a signatory of the Millennium Development Goal (MDG) which highlighted the fact that it is the responsibility of the central and state governments to provide healthcare to every individual. Unfortunately, India is far from providing universal healthcare coverage. Not only have the improvements been slow, but also India is far behind in terms of health indicators, including most developing countries and the few least developed countries. The World Health Organization (WHO) reports that a health system should strengthen the health status of patients, families, and local communities. It must protect the population of the country from health threats and destructive financial consequences caused by innumerable diseases. The health system must provide equal access to human health services and ensure the participation of local communities in decisions that affect their health and health systems. Access to medical professionals, administration, procurement, distribution of equipment and drugs, funding mechanisms, and information generation are the key factors that underlie system failure in low-income countries. A functioning health system is a prerequisite for good healthcare in any country.

2

HEALTH FINANCING IN INDIA

Scholars like Liaropoulos & Goranitis define funding for healthcare as, "A set of ways to raise funds, allocate, and spend the money needed to replicate activities related to promoting, protecting, and improving health."[1] Access to healthcare with equity and accessibility to everyone is closely linked to the financing of healthcare services. However, India's health financing structure has aggravated due to inadequate availability, poor quality services, and most importantly, unequal access. The countries that provide affordable healthcare and equity in accessing the services have developed the healthcare system with public finance funding two-thirds of healthcare spending. In developed countries, these public financings are through state revenue or social insurance. All OECD countries, excluding the USA, have a health-financing mechanism to finance healthcare.[2] In these countries, 85% of financing is contributed from public resources like taxes, social insurance or national insurance that ensures over 90 percent of the population have access to healthcare. Developing countries like India are still reliant on out-of-pocket payments. In India, the missing link is the gap between rural and urban hierarchy along with budget allocation based on regions.

Health is a fundamental right of man and a target of society worldwide. It can be defined as "A state of complete physical, mental and social well-being and not merely the absence of disease or infirmity." However, India is one of the major countries in which diseases are not yet under control. The current healthcare system in India has significant loopholes based on socio-economic status, social class, gender, and region. Rural healthcare is in a deplorable state as 74% of the doctors serve in urban areas. Due to a lack of hygienic hospitals, beds, access to clean drinking water, sufficient housing facilities most doctors are very sparse in rural territories. India's inhabitants are burdened with a significant portion of the world's disease but have only limited healthcare staff, and financial resources are a constraint. Of the 5 million children under the age of 5 who died in 2020, 99% lived in low and middle-income countries. Effective health services could have avoided two-thirds of these deaths— adequate birth care, vaccines, antibiotics, and other such basic steps.

Despite having government programs and healthcare advancements, India still accounts for 20% of maternal mortality deaths in the world. The Infant Mortality Rate (IMR) is at 26.6, which is the highest in India when compared to other developing countries. The Indian political economy of healthcare puts India in the category of the most privatized health sector in the world. The main mechanism of financing healthcare in India is out-of-pocket expenditure. Out of 3.3% of GDP spent on the healthcare sector, 31.28% is publicly financed, 4 % is from social insurance, 12.68% private insurance, and the remaining 52 % being out-of-pocket expenditure. Thus, increasing the role of government health expenditure will be critical if India is to enhance health results and access equity.

Major Problems in the Healthcare Sector

The problems in the healthcare system can be widely split into three issues— (a) *Inequity problems on health*— The health effects of social and economic inequality are discerning. Poverty, resulting from social and economic inequality in a community, is harmful to population health. The health result indicators (mortality, morbidity, and life expectancy) are all affected directly by inequality in a specified population. Table 1 shows that India was enveloped in a decline in health during the period 1950 to 1971, as the values talk so high. The trend persisted with the gradual decline in health indicator values. The annual pace of development decreases after every ten years. From Average Annual Growth Rate values, all indicators showed a decreasing trend with the rate of death falling twice the rate of birth, and the same scenario followed in other indices.

Table 1. Healthcare Indicators in India

Indicator /Year	Birth Rate	Death Rate	Infant Mortality Rate	Maternal Mortality Ratio	Total Fertility Rate
1951	40.8	25.1	148	1321	6
1961	38.7	20.6	129	1180	5.9
1971	36.9	14.9	120	853	5.2
1981	33.9	12.5	110	810	4.5
1991	29.5	9.8	80	424	3.6
2001	23.8	7.6	58	254	2.9
2011	21.7	6.9	44	197	2.5
2021	16.4	9.5	25	97	2

(*Source: Indian Health Statistics Report 2019-2020 & Statista Search Department, 2023*)

(b) *Socio-economic problems* – The state of the economy has a direct impact on a country's health. The infrastructure of health care relies directly on financial strength. The latest economic policy changes have had a definite impact on India's healthcare. A program of economic policy reforms to achieve macroeconomic stability and greater economic growth rates was introduced in 1991. Since the launch of India's financial reforms in 1991, the Indian economy has maintained an average annual growth rate of more than 6%. Growth in GDP in 2003-04 was around 7.5%. Table 2 sheds light on health spending per capita. India's health expenditure in 2000 was $20, rising to $40 in 2007 and $63 in 2012, while China was $43 to $108, and $123. Policies in the health sector in India tended to stress the need to reduce population growth. Stabilizing population growth is important for a big nation such as India, as there are connections between the general population health status and population growth rates. Their health and social status are among the worst in the globe in many Indian states where stabilization of population growth is not a concern. Poverty illnesses continue to influence over half of the population while degrading the environment; occupational hazards and fresh contagious diseases such as AIDS have a severe effect on the population.

Table 2. Per Capita Health Expenditure

Country	Per Capita Total Expenditure at Average Expenditure Rate US $			Per Capita Govt. Expenditure on Health at Average Expenditure Rate in US $		
	2000	2012	2020	2000	2012	2020
India	20	63	57	5	38	21
China	43	123	583	9.45	159	319
Brazil	267	879	701	107	361	313
Australia	1728	4345	5901	1155	3489	4431
USA	4703	8987	11702	2032	4567	6643
Canada	2082	5467	5619	140	3905	4212

(*Source: WHO Statistics Report 2021*)

(c) *Political instability* – India is not a participatory democracy but a representative one. Once the elections are over, for every major decision, the politicians who run the central and state governments don't really need to return to the electorate. Thus, in the five years between one election and another, there is hardly any way for people to express their views on any public choice. There are a number of gaps in the development process left by the government in India owing to the intention or absence of resources. Most Indian politicians are reluctant to make tough but healthy choices because voting policies dominate the agenda. Equality and social justice are an inevitable topic in the process. The political stability should be strong and continuous over at least one to two decades in order to bring about any significant change in the scheme.

Methods to Fund Healthcare in India

There are three major ways to fund healthcare in India— (a) *Social*

Health Insurance – Today's total employment in India is estimated at 400 million people, of which only 28 million are in the organized industry, covered by social security legislation, including social insurance.[3] The largest of these is the Employees' State Insurance Corporation (ESIS), which covers 8 million employees, including family members, and provides health insurance to 33 million persons. The ESIS Corporation spends Rs 12 billion annually on healthcare for its members averaging Rs 365 per beneficiary. This effectively covers 3.2 percent of the population. About half percent of the population is covered through the Central Government Health Scheme (CGHS). The annual spending of the CGHS is Rs 2 billion, with an average of Rs 450 per beneficiary. While these social insurance schemes have been operating for a long time, their reputation is at stake, and large-scale out-sourcing to the private sector is taking place.

The government employees of Indian Railways, defense services, and the telegraph department have significant health care services for their employees, which amounts to Rs 16 billion per annum and averages to Rs 1,150 per beneficiary. The special welfare funds have been set up by the acts of parliament for specific ethnic groups, including selected unorganized sectors like plantation workers, construction workers, mine workers, load workers, etc., that includes benefits of healthcare, education, housing, and water supply. This welfare fund is estimated at about Rs 24 billion per year, averaging Rs 3000 per worker per year.

The Indian government had also introduced social security schemes from time to time, including health coverage for various groups of the population, especially the underprivileged or below poverty line clusters in the unorganized segment like the Krishi Shramik Samajik Sanstha Yojana, National Family benefit scheme, National Social Assistance Program, National Maternity benefit scheme, handloom workers thrift, health & group insurance, agricultural workers central scheme, Jayashree Bima Yojana, National Illness Assistance fund, state govt welfare funds and state illness funds etc. However, these schemes are not offered on a regular basis and are not guaranteed for the next year of the scheme.

It can be seen that only 10 percent of the country's population has some type of social insurance cover for health through their employment.

(b) Private Health Insurance – The recent phenomenon was

studied in an organized way in the mid-eighties through the public sector insurance companies called Private Health Insurance. Prior to that, these private insurance companies provided group insurance schemes for their selected clients that covered a trivial number of employees and their families. Private health insurance picked up momentum gradually and entered the growth phase around 1998, but even today, it covers just over 12% of the population. The public sector insurance companies' gross annual premiums of Rs 10 billion for the medical policies from 10 million insured lives. In the last few years, some private insurance companies have also entered the fray, but they are as yet very small players having less than 10 percent of the market share.

(c) *Mutual Healthcare Insurance* – Mutual healthcare insurance scheme constitutes a fair distribution of the costs of care among different social groups. It includes risk-pooling initiatives by sharing costs among the healthy and the sick, leading to insurance schemes as a substitute for private health insurance. It also covers risk-sharing initiatives across wealth and income involving public policy decisions on progressive taxation, merit, subsidy, and cross-subsidization by dual pricing. Risk-pooling within private voluntary insurance schemes has become inevitable in all countries because of the double burden of sickness and to ensure that financial costs of treatment do not become an excessive burden relative to incomes. While mutual healthcare insurance has obvious advantages, it can have side-effects of inaccessibility and inefficient risk-selecting, resulting in a welfare loss to social groups.

The Different Types of Frameworks to Analyze Healthcare in India

Countries face a myriad of health-related problems related to poverty, lack of access to basic resources, rapid industrialization, urbanization, demographic change, and technological development. The way to understand and study the challenges in the healthcare system is through an analytical framework. There are several frameworks that can be used to study and analyze the challenges in the healthcare system. The "Actors" framework, which classifies four significant actors in a health scheme, is an early framework: suppliers, payers, regulators, and served population.[4] The other widely used framework is the analysis of a country's "national health accounts" (NHA).[5] These accounts meticulously categorize the kinds and purposes of all spending in a healthcare system produced by/to all actors. The WHO has defined the framework of a healthcare system in terms of its basic building blocks.[6] These include service delivery of effective, safe, quality personal and non-personal interventions; An adequate number of the health workforce, knowledgeably trained, and fairly distributed; a health information system that produces, analyzes, and disseminates reliable and timely information; medical products and technologies that are safe, efficacious, cost-effective, and accessible; a financing system that raises adequate funds to ensure the population can use needed services and is protected from financial catastrophe; and governance and oversight of the above. All six building blocks are viewed as essential for developing a health care system.

Two further frameworks concentrate on evaluating the dynamics of the development of the healthcare system. The first discusses trends over time in the price, access, and quality/outcome dimensions of the iron triangle across countries.[7] The framework here examines health expenditures per capita, percent of GDP spent on healthcare, insurance coverage, hospital utilization, and expenditures per capita, physician visits per capita, and such outcomes as life expectancy at birth, infant mortality, and disability days. Insights into the development of health care systems are obtained from cross-border comparisons between these trends. The second framework demonstrates the interrelationship of cost, access, and quality. The "healthcare quadrilemma" model examines the efforts to address problems in access to healthcare by extending insurance coverage to previously uncovered segments of the population that have multiple downstream effects. These include financial incentives to manufacturers and producers to invest more in technological research and development (R&D) since the costs of innovation are more likely to be covered.

These frameworks are applied in the Indian health system to analyze the challenges and propose the guiding principles for the development of the healthcare system with variations in the models. There is a widespread absence of knowledge among the population of sophisticated insurance schemes, medical technologies, and infrastructure due to the low literacy rate and educational level of the country. At present, private insurance premiums are not affordable. There is also a lack of governmental regulation and supplier sector supervision that is delaying quality assurance and enhancement of health care in India. If the government spends more on public healthcare, it will immensely benefit commoners. Higher wages and appropriate living conditions in rural areas will enable medical staff and doctors to serve there. More expenditure will help public hospitals to acquire medicines, clean water supply, electricity, ambulances, hospital beds so that they are functionable when the need arises. With adequate funding and availability of skilled manpower, more public health facilities can be opened to serve the masses. Fundings can also lead to the free treatment of the poor and needy. In addition to free treatment, the government can also provide health insurance to the marginalized groups of people so that they can avail treatment even in private hospitals. Strict regulations regarding the quality of resources will ensure proper access to healthcare.

Apart from government fundings, impact investment is a new dynamic phenomenon that has sparked enthusiasm far and wide. Not only does impact investing help in the healthcare sector, but also in tackling food security, education, and climate change. Social investing or Impact investing is a new charity finance tool that has proven to be far more beneficial than donations. The Global Impact Investing Network defines impact investing as — "Impact investments are investments made with the intention to generate beneficial, measurable social & environmental impact alongside a financial return. Impact investments can be made in both emerging and developed markets and target a range of returns from below market to market rate, depending on the investor's strategic goals."[9]

On the other hand, donation or charity is not a sustainable model. Donations are viewed as the process of investing money for a community that does not include yourself. Most people don't even know how much their donations would be utilized. Moreover, there is no return on investment when you simply donate or offer charitable services. However, with investment, a loan is paid back and can be utilized whenever the need arises. Since grants and donations are shrinking, investment models should exert a more pronounced force on the charity world. It is important to build the social investment market thoughtfully and help charities understand the potential for social investment.

3

THE DIFFERENT SOCIAL ENDOWMENT MODELS

An endowment can be defined as a donation of money or property to a non-profit organization that uses the investment profits for a specific purpose. It is known as the sum of a non-profit institution's investable assets, also referred as its principal or corpus, which is intended to be utilized for activities consistent with the donor's wishes. Endowments are intended to preserve the principal while allowing the investment profits to be used for charitable purposes. The creation of an endowment from a donor's funds is subject to two conditions— First, the donation must remain intact, or the principal sum of the donation must not be used indefinitely. Second, the funds donated must be invested. The endowment is usually structured in a way that the principal is held unchanged while the investment income is available for use, or such that a portion of the principal is released each year, allowing the donation to have a longer effect than if it were expended all at once. The endowment in Islamic civilization is known as Shariah-based endowment or waqf, and it is based on the principle of Islamic law.

The Shariah-based Endowment/Waqf

Shariah-based endowment or waqf is an innovative method in implementing affordable healthcare in India. As per the global statistics, more than 700 million people are striving under extremely unfortunate circumstances.[1] Most people struggle to even meet their basic needs such as food, sanitation, shelter, clean water etc. Thus, through waqf, charity can be channelized for the benefit of poor people. It can alleviate poverty, improve the quality of health services, and provide quality education to the underprivileged. The ultimate objectives of Shariah (maqasid al-shariah) are based on compassion and are entrusted to the benefits of the individual and society, and its rules are structured to preserve these benefits and promote the improvement and perfection of the conditions of life on earth. The Quran expresses this when it identifies the most important object of Muhammad's (PBUH) prophethood in terms like: "We sent thee not, but as a mercy for all creatures" and "O mankind, there has to come to you instruction from your Lord and healing for what is in the heart and guidance and mercy for the believers." Other conditions in the Quran and Sunnah that aim to create justice, eradicate prejudice, and relieve suffering, which is reflected in the realization of benefit, illustrate the two objectives of mercy (rahmah) and guidance (huda). Justice is both a manifestation of God's mercy and a Shariah goal in and of itself. As a result, maqasid al-shariah is the branch of Islamic teaching that explains why such rulings are made. One of these pearls of wisdom is about "strengthening social solidarity."

The institution of *infaq* is one of the key foundations of the Islamic economic system. *Infaq* is described as "giving away for the benefit of society and its members, including the giver and his or her family." Every asset, beyond what a human being requires, is an asset or a mal of Allah and must be expended in his direction. The word *'infaq'* is used in conjunction with the phrase 'Fi Sabil Allah', which means giving for Allah's pleasure or charitable purposes. It contributes to the public good with the aim of worshiping Allah according to Shariah values. It is similar to *sadaqah*, which is essentially self-sacrifice in order to achieve Allah's approval. From a religious perspective, there are many forms of *infaq*, one of which is voluntary expenditure motivated by religious motives. This form of *infaq* can be divided into two categories: ongoing spending and one-time spending. Giving for charitable causes, such as assisting the needy by providing cash to purchase food, is one-time spending. Waqf, on the other hand, is a running-stream type of *infaq* that focuses on revenues or services. Irrevocability, perpetuity, and inalienability are the most significant features of waqf.

The Role of Endowment in Healthcare

In this chapter, our key takeaways will be an elaboration of the two social endowment models, and how they contribute towards healthcare in India— A waqf based model for financing healthcare & a cash waqf based model for financing social enterprises. Researchers like Swift, T. & Zadek, S. have addressed the types of health centers supported by waqf and drawn attention to healthcare, service growth, and funding for the creation of integrated medical neighborhoods. Several educational institutions are surrounded by people who assist in the execution of various ventures, all of which were funded by endowment funds and catered for sick students and workers under the supervision of physicians, pharmacists, and medical students. Waqf's main goal is to collect funds in order to support a variety of programs that benefit the entire community. Many large businesses have started to endow cash or return to philanthropy in order to help the needy in recent years. The Bill and Melinda Gates Foundation, established in 2000, included the William H. Gates Health Foundation, and it was one of the first to do so. Indian businessman Azim Premji established the Azim Premji Foundation in 2001 to promote reform in the fields of healthcare and education. Premji's contributions to the Foundation's endowment, valued at USD 21 billion, made it one of the world's largest foundations. The Azim Premji Endowment Fund owns 13.6% of the promoter's shares in Wipro and is entitled to all profits generated by promoter shares.

In India, the value of assets held in Islamic endowments is enormous. According to the Report on the Social, Economic, and Educational Status of India's Muslim Community, more than 490,000 Islamic endowments are registered. The total area under-endowed land assets are estimated to be 600,000 acres, with 80% of it in rural India and the rest in major cities. The book value of these properties is estimated to be USD 1 billion, while the market value is estimated to be USD 20 billion. At the same time, endowed asset income is low, with an approximate annual income of USD 27 million, or 2.7 % value. These large waqf infrastructures are under the Ministry of Minorities Affairs, Government of India, but waqf boards formed at the provincial or state level have considerable autonomy. By forming local committees, these waqf boards work for the management, control, and security of the waqf assets. There are currently thirty waqf boards operating across the country. The Central Waqf Council is a statutory body set up by the Indian government to advise it on matters relating to the functioning of Waqf Boards and the proper administration of the *awqaf* in the country. Waqf properties in India benefit greatly from property development mechanisms, which help them become more revenue-generating and sustainable waqf properties. In this model, Waqf boards and custodians enter into investment or development agreements with organizations to develop the waqf properties into hospitals. The organizations provide the investable funds as well as the specialized knowledge needed to improve these existing waqf assets. The revenue streams generated by these established waqf assets are used to provide healthcare services to people, either through the renovation of existing facilities, the establishment of new facilities, or the use of creative healthcare delivery methods such as mobile treatment services. Hazrat Bismillah Shah (HBS) Hospital, 100 bedded hospitals located in Bengaluru, India, is built on waqf property that provides healthcare services on a non-profit basis. The land is owned by the Wakf Board and was endowed by Hazrat Bismillah Shah, a religious and pious personality.

Waqfs of various forms, including cash waqf, corporate waqf, and waqf shares, have been effective in funding health systems, providing medical services to the poor and vulnerable, organizing various welfare schemes, and providing social entrepreneur growth programs. Waqf has aided medical and healthcare services in communities. An Islamic medical endowment, on the other hand, did not only focus on offering health care services to society; it also offered opportunities for science students studying medicine at the University. Medical centers were funded by endowment funds, medical care, procedures, drugs, and food that they offered were provided for free in exchange for the endowments that Muslims monitored for these humanitarian purposes. In the growth of hospitals, the pious endowment of *awqaf* has made a significant contribution. Many hospitals and health facilities in the country and overseas, which serve both Muslim and Non-Muslim patients, were constructed and paid for by a waqf institution. The salaries of doctors, the tuition of eligible medical students, medical books, medical colleges, and health facilities have all relied on funds raised through waqf. Unique *awqaf* have also been developed for specialized medical schools for chemistry research as well as the payment of food and medication for hospital patients. The patients were also granted financial assistance so that they could obtain free care. Since the position of hospitals operated by *awqaf* was not limited to providing care, waqf has had a positive impact on the advancement of medical sciences.

Historical Development of Cash Waqf Model

Besides the waqf based model, cash based waqf is also another type of endowment that is helpful in funding the healthcare system. Cash waqf is the confinement of a certain amount of money by individuals, institutions or organizations for the purpose of mobilizing public funds. It is considered as a way to accomplish modern macro-economic development, reduce an organization's debt and budget deficit, and fund development projects. According to one meaning, cash waqf refers to a founder's commitment of a sum of money and the dedication of its usufruct in perpetuity to prescriptive purposes. Cash waqf is also defined as the restriction of a sum of money by a founder (individuals, businesses, institutions, corporations, or public or private organizations) and the commitment of its usufruct in perpetuity to the benefit of society. Hafsah, one of Prophet Muhammad S.A.W. 's wives, is said to have purchased jewels worth 20,000 dirham and dedicated them to the women of the al-Khattab family lineage. Imam Malik Ibn Anas was the first prominent classical scholar to be credited with allowing cash waqf in a clear and unambiguous manner (93-179AH). He went on to say that such cash waqf funds could be lent to citizens as revolving loans, with the borrower obligated to repay only the amount borrowed.

The revival of the practice of cash waqf can be traced back to the Ottoman Empire in modern times (1301-1922 CE). The Turks are rightfully credited with popularizing cash waqf. However, as the

Ottoman Empire fell apart in the 19th century, the tradition of cash waqf practically died out. In 1999, it reappeared in the Sultanate of Oman and the State of Kuwait, and then in the United Arab Emirates in 2001. Cash waqf was also permitted by Malaysia's National Fatwa Council in 2007. The practice of cash waqf has flourished and spread across the Muslim world since then. Cash waqf plays a significant role in many healthcare services such as building hospitals and clinic chains, offering dialysis centers, dialysis machines, and health services such as mobile clinics, and treating deserving patients with the bare minimum of care and medication. In many countries, the institution of waqf has been revived in the twenty-first century, as has the development of cash waqf in general. Many cash waqf systems have recently been implemented in various countries.

A funding model based on the concept of partnership (*mudarbha*) was proposed where the usage of cash waqf could be extended to enterprise financing.[2] The model also suggested that cash waqf could be used as a financial instrument for small business owners based on Islamic microfinance institutions. However, Islamic microfinance institutions faced their own set of challenges as their existing procedures converge with mainstream practices. Furthermore, Islamic microfinance institutions mostly use debt-based financing, which is similar to traditional interest-based financing. Moreover, due to the prevalence of *murabaha* (cost plus mark-up) practices and administrative costs that are equivalent to usury (*riba*), the operations of Islamic microfinance institutions in several nations tend to be extravagant.

Another funding model proposed that cash waqf could help small-medium enterprises overcome their lack of access to traditional financial institutions.[3] The model suggested that enterprises can extend their commercial ventures by partnering with cash waqf institutions and properly using and investing their cash waqf assets. However, cash waqf institutions suffer a number of barriers that make the cash waqf institutions ineffective. Internal restrictions, such as a lack of qualified human resources, transparent reporting, and rigorous recordkeeping, are mostly to blame. Furthermore, external constraints, such as the lack of uniform waqf enactments, have had an impact on the efficiency of cash waqf institutions.

The author, Tohirin, had developed a Cash waqf model for

empowerment of small businesses. He presented the concept of Cash waqf organization based on three steps — Firstly, the donations should be mobilized as a fund-raising method. Secondly, the accumulated funds should be used for generating income through portfolio investment. Thirdly, the benefit/income generated should be distributed among the beneficiaries. The income distribution can be used in many ways. It can be used for charity to needy people. It can also be used for empowering businesses with financial troubles by contracting with them for Islamic modes of financing such as *mudharaba*, *musharaka* or *murabaha*. The author believed that Cash Waqf had potential in empowering the small business because most small businesses were not in position to fulfill the loan criteria of formal financial institutions for obtaining funds. Due to its important role, the Cash waqf model can be the best source of finance for them under Islamic financial system.

There are other shariah based endowment models too that fund for healthcare. One such model is ICWME-I, which is the integrated cash waqf micro-enterprise investment model.[4] It provides financial assistance via a cash waqf fund and entails a collaborative agreement between Islamic non-profit organizations, primarily waqf institutions, and small businesses. However, it has not been experimentally validated and tested in the study, which is one of its primary flaws. Furthermore, the ICWME-I model is specially designed for the human capital development of micro-enterprises. The Venture Philanthropy of Waqf Model (VPWM) model is proposed in combination with the establishment of sustainable waqf businesses.[5] Instead of focusing on financial return maximization as traditional venture capitalists do, VPWM's major goal is to achieve and maximize social good.

In this VPWM model, the fund is endowed to the administrator, who subsequently invests in social enterprises with a strong potential for social impact. According to the VPWM model, a social enterprise does not just organize its social entrepreneurial operations to become self-sustaining but also to channel contributions to society. However, this model engages a three-stage life cycle, and asset building is the first phase taking around five to ten years. Moreover, in this model, the administrator has the power to decide whether the waqf fund should be reinvested or distributed to the beneficiaries.

Apart from the VPWM model, the CWFI model (cash waqf

financial institution) was proposed to assist small and medium-sized enterprises with interest-free loans in order to commence their businesses.[6] Micro-enterprises have shown a high level of preparedness to accept the CWFI model as a source of financial and human capital growth. This financing model suggests investing only 50 percent to ensure the continuity of waqf capital money. However, only 10 percent of the remaining 50 percent can be put in a partnership arrangement to supply capital, but not necessarily participate in the business. Secondly, CWFI acts as a trustee and gives the micro-enterprises the capital for a set amount of time in exchange for an agreement to split the profits in a predetermined proportion. In the event of a loss, the CWFI bears it, thereby discouraging the trustees from investing and supporting the micro-enterprises.

Thus, in this chapter we have learnt about the different types of cash waqf models demonstrating the possibility of integrating cash waqf and micro-enterprises to effectively address the issue of financing for micro-enterprises. Furthermore, these cash waqf models are waqf funding institutions financing the micro or medium enterprises; although cash waqf institutions are investing into social enterprises, funding in social enterprises is considered a high-risk investment. Secondly, cash waqf institutions do not get involved in the business model of the enterprises, as they support only the funding needs of the enterprises. The results of only financing the enterprises, therefore, do not guarantee the financial return of cash waqf institutions, and the investment to social enterprises remains less attractive. Moreover, there is a deficiency of well-developed and tested models for social enterprises, specifically with the business model through cash waqf as equity capital funding.

4

EVERYTHING ABOUT SOCIAL ENTERPRISE

The Indian political economy of healthcare in India puts India in the category of the most privatized health sector in the world. The main mechanism of financing healthcare in India is out-of-pocket expenditure. Thus, increasing the role of government health expenditure will be critical if India is to enhance health results and access equity. In addition, the healthcare system will have to be organized and controlled within a universal access framework. As India has its own distinctiveness, any healthcare system will have to be designed with keeping financing in mind. The 75th round of National Sample Survey 2017-18 shows a profile of India's present financing system and spending and presents trends in health expenditure over the past three decades. It is quite clear that public healthcare finances are weakening and that private expenditure is becoming even higher. Given the dominant presence of the private sector in health, multiple governments in India have involved the private sector, for-profit as well as social enterprise with it to satisfy the increasing requirements of the population in terms of health care. The strategic involvement of the social enterprise enhances the capital, efficiency, responsibility, quality, and accessibility of the entire health scheme.

Over the last two decades, social enterprises have attracted academic interest in a variety of fields, including entrepreneurship, management, economic growth, non-profit, and public policy. Robert Owen, an eighteenth-century merchant, is credited with establishing one of the first known social enterprises, and Florence Nightingale, a late-nineteenth-century social entrepreneur, revolutionized healthcare conditions. Social enterprises in Turkey have their roots in the Ottoman Empire's tradition of foundations offering people health services. It spanned from the 14th century through the early twentieth centuries. However, since the late 1990s, unmet socio-economic needs have prompted an increase in the number of social enterprises to grow around the world. Governments have also aided this expansion, recognizing the significant importance of social enterprises in addressing social issues. Scholars refer to social enterprises as "social projects", "social entrepreneurs", "community-led social ventures", "community-based enterprises", "social entrepreneurial ventures", and "social entrepreneurial organizations". However, since "social enterprise", defined as an entity that engages in commercial activities in order to achieve social goals, is the most widely used concept in the literature, it is used in this study.

Social enterprises differ from for-profit businesses in terms of their features. The major differences between them are their goals and beliefs. Benefit maximization is the operational objective of for-profit businesses, while the operational goal of social organizations is to increase social-oriented benefits. Social enterprises are more successful suppliers of public services and growth markets that are restricted by formal-sector enterprises. The problem is in figuring out how to conceptualize and quantify the success of social enterprises in the distribution of public and private services, as well as what metrics to use. The performance of a social enterprise is measured in more than just financial terms; a non-financial perspective is also important to consider. It is mandatory to consider the social value and change as a means of developing appropriate steps of social enterprise. However, the challenge that social enterprises face is balancing their social and financial objectives. Social enterprises usually face challenges in obtaining start-up and investment capital, setting prices and controlling cash flow, and scaling their businesses. Although the social purpose remains the heart and soul of the organization, social enterprises report that organizations struggle to generate economic value that sustains them during the establishment period and beyond.

Examples of Social Enterprises

The largest social enterprise sector in the world–UK Health Secretary Andrew Lansley, in 2010, described the dream to create the 'greatest social enterprise sector in the world' in England by "liberating foundation trusts and providing services to NHS workers". The 'Right to Provide' plan was soon revealed, offering front-line primary care staff in England the ability to set up social enterprises to provide a variety of primary and community care services, ranging from general practitioners and nursing services to sexual health, epilepsy, dermatology, physiotherapy, child health surveillance, and minor surgery. The program has so far created forty-five new social enterprises, ranging from small, six-person enterprises to those employing more than 1000 people with a turnover of £ 100 m or more. One notable example is Salford Health Matters, a community interest company (CIC-a kind of UK social enterprise legal structure) set up by former NHS employees to provide essential medical services to some 30 000 people living in Greater Manchester's Salford area. All the income on the services they offer to the National Health Service under contract (free at the point of delivery) is reinvested in health and for the benefit of the Salford community. In addition to offering community health programs, they have a clear business goal of delivering new resources and incentives for 3 000 individuals most in need to tackle the determinants of ill-health in the following areas: homelessness, fuel deprivation, mental wellbeing, and social isolation.

Aravind Eye Care System, an Indian social enterprise, the world's largest eye care provider, attracts wealthier patients who pay market rates and then provides the same services at a highly subsidized or free rate for the poorer 70 percent of their patients. They define differential pricing by the patient's choice of facilities and the type of lens to be implanted in the eye, not by the standard of care the patient gets. All patients receive the same medical care, regardless of their ability to pay, but paying patients can choose soft lenses and sleep in private rooms, while non-paying patients receive the basic hard lens and sleep in open dormitories on mats. This strategy, called price targeting, is an efficient way to determine financial need, as those who can afford private rooms and soft lenses are far more likely to select them. Aravind Eye Care System also increased productivity by re-engineering its operating rooms to allow surgeons to operate alternately on two tables by switching from one case to the next. While one operation is underway, the next patient is trained by a team of 4 nurses and paramedical staff. This innovation enables Aravind to perform a cataract operation in 10 minutes-one-third of the 30-minute industry standard. Given the shared patient room, their infection rates are 4 per 10 000 patients, which is better than the reported 6 per 10 000 in the UK. Aravind also monitors surgical results by the surgeon and offers assistance to those below average, which leads to the quality of care improvements.

Role of Social Enterprises in the Healthcare System

In recent years, social enterprise as an alternative form of delivering healthcare has obtained a lot of attention. Different types of social enterprises have different effects on various aspects of health, such as fostering a sense of ownership and control, improving physical and social conditions, and giving or facilitating meaningful employment. Social enterprises are private organizations founded by communities engaged in the supply of goods and services specifically for the benefit of communities and bearing high autonomy and full responsibility for their economic situation. These private healthcare providers have been encouraged to enter the healthcare sector, particularly in India, on the premise that they are more innovative and responsive than their public sector counterparts. However, in India, out-of-pocket expenditure accounts for 70 percent of total health expenditure. Therefore, this raises the question of whether private healthcare providers are affordable. Furthermore, the private healthcare providers may create a social divide by allowing the wealthy to receive medical care while the poor remain sick.

Collaboration in healthcare can handle rising healthcare user expectations as well as existing healthcare concerns, such as the rise in chronic diseases and population aging, all of which necessitate increasing collaboration across healthcare players to be adequately addressed. It can also lead to improved resource creation, communication, and coordination. Thus, resulting in improved healthcare performance. However, close cooperation is critical for healthcare development because it brings together healthcare stakeholders to accomplish common and improved goals. Also, collaborative healthcare involves interdependence teams sharing power and responsibility. Another important issue is who collaborates such as professionals (including clinicians such as nurses, medical doctors), non-clinical professionals (such as accountants and administrative staff, among others), and patients, suppliers of healthcare products, and policy makers. The available studies have focused on one or two stakeholders in defining the collaboration. However, in recent decades, there has been a push to reorient health care towards a more viable and sustainable means of organizing such healthcare activities, resulting in the emergence of social enterprise.

Social enterprises have been deemed as an affordable means of delivering health services. The researchers looked into the mechanisms and pathways via which social enterprises could be used as a public health intervention. The data collected revealed that social enterprises might have a favorable impact on affordable healthcare, although only five studies were included in the final analysis. Additionally, the study focused on "work integration social enterprises" that aimed to provide employment for people who are disengaged or disadvantaged from the mainstream labor market. The objective of the study was not to compare the outcomes of social enterprises to those of traditional healthcare providers; rather, it wanted to know how social enterprise activity affected health outcomes by addressing social factors. However, the study concluded that social enterprise could improve skills and employability while also enhancing self-reliance, developing affordable healthcare services, raising social capital, and improving health behaviors.

Although social enterprises can deliver affordable and accessible healthcare services to all segments of the population, it does not always guarantee that the organization is sustainable as it requires specific ways to run the organization and not just have a social mission. Therefore, sustainability of social enterprise is important, particularly in the healthcare sector in India, as inequalities in access to quality health services and health outcomes are higher in the low and middle-income countries, India being one of them. One of the most important obstacles that social enterprises face around the world is achieving financial sustainability in order to fund and maintain healthcare projects over long periods of time. Though the definition of social enterprise puts emphasis on the social value, the poor financial performance of social enterprises is punished more readily than poor social performance.

Another challenge arises in terms of measuring social value. These factors constrain social enterprises' access to traditional finance. However, new sources of capital for social enterprises known as "impact investment" have emerged as a result of recent innovations in social investment instruments. This new type of finance is funded by investors looking for chances to invest in organizations that generate social value while still making a profit. It is noted that social enterprises that offer significant social value without generating positive discounted cash flows are often funded through government grants and philanthropic donations. However, in the recent decade, a growing class of impact investors have supported some of these social enterprises through typical social financing strategies. It has also been noticed that an increasing number of investors and investment organizations have turned to social enterprises to boost their income while also maximizing their social impact. This innovative social financing is reflected in the healthcare sector's rising earned income revenues resulting in the financial sustainability of social enterprises.

Funding Sources for Social Enterprises

Social enterprises have had access to various social finance instruments in recent years. In general, social enterprises have two options for social funding: (a) Equity financing: from organizations and/or individuals that want a share of the business's profits. (b) Credit or debt financing: from organizations and/or individuals who intend the principal amount and interest to be repaid on a predetermined schedule. One of the best instruments for dealing with the financing issue is equity or the ownership interest of shareholders in a company. Holding equity in the company does not imply that investors have a say in the company's management and how it functions. It also does not give investors discounts on any goods and services from the company. However, some benefits come with owning equity in a company, including invitations to shareholder meetings where investors can express their opinions on important matters affecting the company. For-profit companies use equity to access startup funds when starting a new business. However, a lack of access to equity finance is seen as a significant barrier to growth and development. Off late, there have been reports of a few social enterprises experimenting with different types of equity as a source of funding.[1] There are two types of equity opportunities open to social enterprises: a) Internal equity sources b) External equity sources.

According to many academics, creating internal equity is the best first source.[2] Surpluses from the past are regarded as the best source of equity. Some organizations will use the funds they have amassed over time to launch a new venture. However, since social enterprises seldom have surpluses, such methods are uncommon. Furthermore, federal financial aid is generally withheld from social enterprises with a surplus once they have spent all their funds. Creating a trust fund is another viable choice for social enterprises to overcome the difficulty of developing internal equity. It has been used successfully by several organizations. Eco-Lumber Co-op, for example, creates equity by withdrawing 5% of the money charged for products and services bought by its members. This money is placed into a trust account and used as collateral for loans. When the loans are repaid, the money kept in trust is usually returned to the members. On the other hand, social enterprises face obstacles such as legal constraints, an unstable flow of funds from internal sources, and a lack of surplus, all of which prohibit them from building internal equity.

In terms of external equity source, grant donations to social enterprises are often considered as a source of equity since they are yet to be repaid. Grants are increasingly being defined as investments focusing on social returns rather than financial gains by funders. Unlike conventional grants used to fund an organization's social services, new grants (also known as philanthro-equity) are being made available for the organization's capacity building, like professional development and training. These grants are based on for-profit management concepts and take advantage of the grantor's enhanced appetite for scalable impacts and better outcome assessment. However, the grant donation could have been a bit more predictable and consistent. It often comes with a set of conditions that may harm the aims and purposes of the organization. To accommodate or satisfy the objectives or requirements of grant donors, some social enterprises may have to adapt or modify their aims or program priorities. A recent study on financing social enterprises argued that impact investments could assist social enterprises in achieving financial sustainability and reducing their reliance on grant donations.[3] However, a growing body of theoretical work analyzes how impact investors with social preferences invest their capital.[4]

In contrast to the previous research, this study looks at the correct time period to encourage social enterprises with an investment rather than a grant. This decision is linked with how well a socially conscious organization is positioned to make a profit. Another study also examined the determination of social financiers to make an investment or a donation.[5] The author focuses on a problem between commercial and socially-minded investors, noting that by reducing the commercial investor's share in a firm, the impact investor can discipline the commercial investor to pursue socially acceptable goals. The previous study concluded that impact investment leads to the financial sustainability of the social enterprise. In recent years, a high-engagement approach to impact investment across a range of social enterprises has emerged in the form of Venture philanthropy.[6] External sources of equity, such as philanthropy-equity and the rise of venture philanthropy, replaced internal equity. With high levels of interaction between the donor and the investee, venture philanthropy provides both access to capital and knowledge between the philanthropist and the organization. To define Venture philanthropy— It is a modern and integrated approach to philanthropy that borrows its name from the traditional business model of venture capital and combines social and financial benefits. Its rapid growth results from social enterprises' demands for large sums of money to address short-term funded investment shortcomings. The aim of establishing venture philanthropy is to build a win-win situation for both the capital provider and the recipient. On the other hand, a conventional venture capitalist may be looking for financial returns, while venture philanthropy may be looking for social returns. Venture philanthropy, commercial ventures, and social venture capital are the three types of non-traditional sources. The three have one thing in common— they all provide support in the hopes of receiving returns that can be used for charitable purposes.

In general, returns are created by commercial activities. Funders may be directly involved in the entire process as entrepreneurs or partners, or they may simply invest without taking a stake in the company. Social enterprises will benefit from this system because the income produced commercially would help to ensure its sustainability. Furthermore, the venture philanthropy fund stays involved for several years if social enterprise business models show scalability. In addition to social enterprises' ability to scale, venture philanthropists are interested in supporting social enterprises with innovative business models that have the potential to create sustainable impact. In the future, venture philanthropy may purposefully assist social enterprises in reaching a proof point that allows social investors to engage at the growth or sustaining stage. The microfinance sector, funded by venture philanthropy, is an example of this transformation. For social enterprises to start their business, equity or investment funding, whether internal or external, is definitely an advantage. However, due to the possible tension between financial shareholder interests and the social goals of the social enterprise, using equity systems can sometimes be contentious. Furthermore, equity holders may want to be active in business management, which could dilute the social goals. This study looks at new financial instruments that social enterprises are using. At different stages of growth, social enterprises, like for-profit businesses, need various forms of funding, and a venture philanthropy form of internal equity source can be best for social enterprises.

Concept of Business Model in Social Enterprise

In addition to impact investment, social enterprises have embraced a modern business model as a potential road to financial sustainability over the last two decades, among other strategies. Several researchers studied business models in social enterprise.[7] However, more research still needs to address frameworks for developing business models in social enterprise, particularly healthcare services. A well-structured financial model is required for financial planning and control through the free flow of capital and cost structure analysis. The financial model of the business model framework consists of six dimensions- The financing or capital model, the revenue model, the pricing model, the expense model, the profit model, and the delivery model. The funding model identifies the sources of capital needed to execute the business model. Social finance is invested in the equity capital of the business model. Social finance as a capital component of the social enterprise business model helps bring financial sustainability to the organization.

In the healthcare sector, business models are constantly under pressure due to population growth, emerging illnesses, demand for quality services, technological innovations, changes in local laws, and changes in players' competitive positions. Healthcare service providers are known as the nodal point of the healthcare system in relation to the various stakeholders in this process— the medical-hospital equipment industry, the pharmaceutical industry, health insurance, public health policy, health professionals, etc. Such relationships foster knowledge and information sharing among these actors, contributing to innovation growth. Healthcare centers are also teaching and researching focal points in various areas and bringing them closer to the development of science and technology. For example, the Health and Wellness Centres under under the Ayushman Bharat Programme have implemented digital health technologies and best practices for primary health care and the Harvard T.H. Chan School of Public Health India Research Center has developed innovative solutions and tools for public health challenges.

Several scholars had looked into social enterprise business models. However, little study has been done on frameworks for developing business models in social enterprises, especially in the context of healthcare services. Researchers had used the business model canvas paradigm in the sense of consumer management models, validating their functionality in the social enterprise. However, they focus on the role of the canvas framework in supporting the adoption of various forms of consumer services instead of addressing business model issues, specifically related to social enterprise. The business model canvas has also been used in the healthcare context of the social enterprise. The business model definition is used to define opportunities for changes in service quality to tackle internal, external, and resource performance in each of the elements of the business model. The later study expanded the concept of the business model further and introduced a new framework for business model development in the social enterprise.[8] Given the difficulties in defining specific components of the business model, this study adopts the viewpoint that the social enterprise's approach informs the business model in place, which further decides the healthcare services activities to be performed.

In early 2020, the Coronavirus pandemic grasped nations across the world. The healthcare systems of countries were already crumbling in figuring out a way to fight the spread of Coronavirus. The medical experts and government sources indicated that only a strong immunity could fight the deadly virus. To develop immunity, one should have a considerable amount of Vitamins in the body. Hence, several people had taken Vitamins & Multi-Vitamins to keep their immunity strong. While on the other hand, underprivileged families struggled to have their daily meals, and to follow the proper Vitamin dosage for the entire family could not be anticipated. However, getting a sufficient amount of Vitamin D was important for the improved resistance against Coronavirus. Hence, GoBizLAB Healthcare, the case social enterprise, had taken the initiative to distribute Vitamin D vials and help in developing the immunity of the underprivileged families. The operation was run by the executive director with a team of four people, but most of the operations of the case social enterprise were managed by two stakeholders.

The case social enterprise is registered as Section 8 Company under the Companies Act 2013. A Section 8 Company is a company (for charitable or not-for-profit purposes) established 'for promoting commerce, art, science, sports, education, research, social welfare, religion, charity, protection of environment or any such other object', provided the profits, if any, or other income is applied for promoting only the objects of the company, and no dividend is paid to its members. The case social enterprise received the funds to deliver the Vitamin D through the donation accumulated on the crowdfunding web portal by the partner NGO, RIDA Foundation - a Mumbai based, non-political, not-for-profit development organization, registered as a trust under Mumbai Public Trust Act, 1950. The partner NGO works with hospitals and healthcare service providers to deliver affordable healthcare services to underprivileged patients. The business model of the case social enterprise represented a traditional healthcare perspective– acting as a medium between donors and patients. The activities were simple— raising the donation from the supporters and providing medical treatment to the underprivileged patients. The medical services from doctors are availed with professional fees and offered to underprivileged patients for free. The business model is represented in graphical format using the Business Model Canvas, as shown in Figure 1:

Figure 1. Business Model Canvas of Social Enterprise

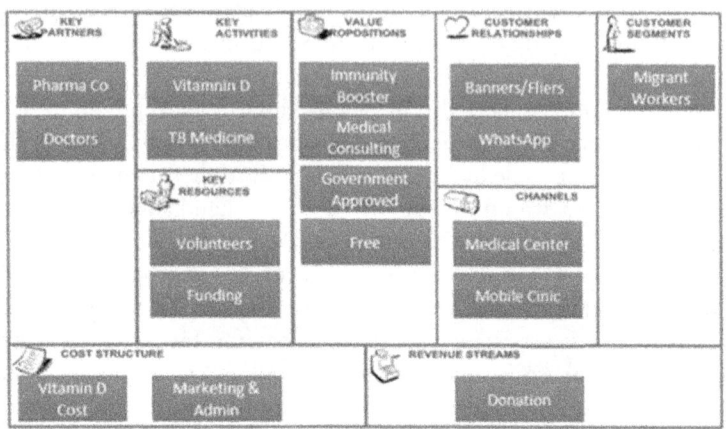

Here's a detailed breakdown of each component:

(a) *Customer Segments:* The customer segment was the migrant workers who were impacted the most during the lockdown period in India due to the COVID-19 pandemic.

(b) *Value Proposition:* The core value proposition was free Vitamin D to the migrant workers. These immunity boosters were offered to the migrant workers under the supervision of government-approved medical doctors.

(c) *Customer Relationship:* This was based on the information fliers and banners. The migrant workers were suggested by various NGOs and communicated with WhatsApp.

(d) *Channels:* There were two channels to distribute the Vitamin D vial to the migrant workers - the physical medical center of the social enterprise based in Kurla, Mumbai & through the medical clinic van serving various slum areas of Mumbai.

(e) *Key Partners:* The pharmaceutical company was the main partner. The social enterprise procured the Vitamin D vial directly from the pharmaceutical company. The medical doctors in the mobile clinic were the delivery partners of the Vitamin D to migrant workers.

(f) *Key Activities:* Activities involved distributing the Vitamin D vial to the migrant workers. The state government also provided free TB medicine to distribute to migrant workers during the pandemic.

(g) *Key Resources:* The main resources were people consisting of

the executive director, one project manager, three trainees, and volunteers responsible for delivering healthcare services.
(h) *Revenue Stream:* The revenue was mainly from donations to social enterprise.
(i) *Cost Structure:* The majority of the cost was that of Vitamin D vial. The salary of stakeholders was fixed cost. The last component was the marketing and administrative cost of delivering the services. The initial Business Model was simple and can be characterized as social intermediaries who procure medical products and services from suppliers and offer them to underprivileged patients. In addition, key activities were executed by the social enterprise, and as a result, the value creation for the patient was mainly created by the social enterprise.

The business process of the case social enterprise had presented a straightforward healthcare service to the underprivileged segment. It provides a social enterprise typology that suggests possible business models. According to the logical structure of social relations between social enterprises, patients, and healthcare services offered, the specific business model that resulted from the nine fundamental types of business models for social enterprises is the type market intermediary model. The model's key advantage is its potential for scalability by reaching out to underprivileged segments in different areas and ensuring a constant focus on the social mission. However, it has certain self-financing limitations. The donation was the only source of revenue, and it was collected through a partner NGO. The entire proceeds of the donations were then utilized to deliver the medical service to the patients.

Figure 2. Social Enterprise Healthcare Services Delivery

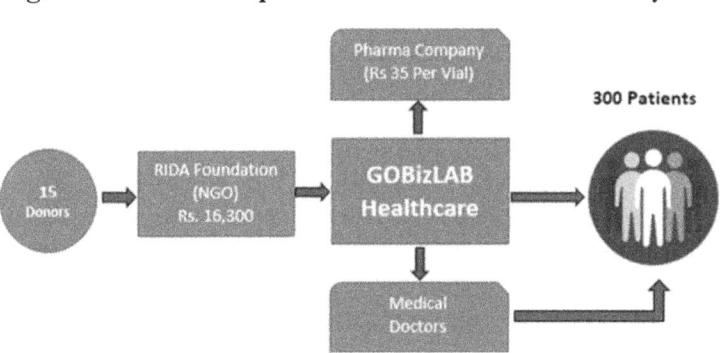

As seen in the diagram, the invoice from the pharmaceutical company and the medical bills from the patient were collected. The review of the profit and loss account statement of the Vitamin D project executed by the social enterprise resulted in zero profit. Therefore, the social enterprise in the example was not financially sustainable. Financial sustainability is considered a prerequisite for successful social investment decision-making and social enterprise success. Obtaining financial sustainability in order to fund and maintain healthcare projects over extended periods of time is one of the most significant challenges that social enterprises face around the world. Given the dynamic, competitive, and volatile economic conditions in which conventional sources of funding are declining, this is a difficult challenge. However, social enterprises fail to secure social investment, which is a complex and challenging issue for many social enterprises. A major risk of relying heavily on external sources of funds is identified in the literature on the financial sustainability of social enterprises. In response, throughout the last two decades, social enterprises have embraced a modern business model as a possible path to financial sustainability, among other methods.

Knowledge Gap: A Panacea for Conducting Research

The sad state of waqf properties in India, as well as the legality of cash waqf, has opened the door for novel approaches to finance the health system through the waqf to be investigated. In many countries, the institution of waqf has been revived in the 21st century like the development of cash waqf in general. Many cash waqfs have recently been practiced in various countries. With its commercial and financial aspects, the cash waqf is more efficient for the benefit of the health system in particular, and for society in general, especially at the macroeconomic level.

The literature review clearly demonstrates that social enterprises face sustainability challenges in both developing and developed countries while fulfilling their social mission through healthcare delivery. Financial and social sustainability issues are frequently highlighted in social enterprise literature. According to the critical study of the literature in this chapter, the most serious sustainability difficulty that social enterprises encounter is financial in nature. Access to capital funding is widely acknowledged as a continuous barrier to social enterprises' survival and growth.[9]

From a literature review on the financial sustainability of social enterprises, it has been observed that social enterprises attempt to achieve financial sustainability through a sustainable business model. Well, the sustainable business model is developed with the process of integrating sustainability into the business model through the business model innovation process. The innovation component of the business model for sustainability of social enterprise is found in the literature in the form of innovative social financing. Social finance is integrated into the social enterprise business model to achieve financial sustainability through the business model change described in the literature.

Despite the fact that a lot of research has been done on several forms of social finance available to social enterprises, it is clear that these studies focus on distinct theories that advise alternative financing.[10] However, there is a dearth of business model literature regarding the financial sustainability of social enterprise through social finance.[11] Furthermore, there is a wealth of literature around social finance and financing of social enterprise, more specifically with shariah-based endowment investment. However, as previously stated, there is limited literature that draws these two areas of "business model" and "shariah-based endowment investment" together. Though, a recent study in 2021 tried to develop a business model to finance social enterprise through cash waqf in generating capital revenue.[12] However, the study has the limitation that the waqf business model was created particularly for producing capital revenue for social enterprises as a waqf superintendent to invest the cash waqf in other permitted businesses. Thus, this study aims to develop a business model of social enterprise through cash waqf investment in the form of equity capital funding to achieve financial sustainability that can provide affordable healthcare services in India. This research bridges this gap and adds value to the existing literature on the business model and social enterprise theory by adding new insights and by being the first research on this level conducted in the context of affordable healthcare in India. It also aids the development of social enterprises in the country by progressing our understanding of how social finance can further support social enterprise growth within India using the waqf investment method of capital funding.

Along with this chapter, the previous two chapters have critically reviewed the most relevant literature pertaining to the financial sustainability of the healthcare social enterprise in India. This chapter explored the concept of social enterprises, discussed the financing of healthcare, analyzed the mechanism of the healthcare financing used among the Indian population, and empirically studied the financial sustainability and business model of the case social enterprise. It is argued that the growing out-of-pocket expense financing of the healthcare system shall be replaced with the involvement of social enterprise to satisfy the increasing requirements of the population in terms of health care. The review of the literature suggested that the strategic involvement of the social enterprise enhances the efficiency, quality, accessibility, and affordability of healthcare services.

This chapter also explored the financial sustainability of the healthcare social enterprise. It is stated that social finance invested as equity capital of the business model could assist social enterprises in achieving financial sustainability. The examination of the third set of literature portrayed gradually emerging research interest in discussing shariah-based endowment (waqf) to include social enterprise financing to achieve the sustainability of the organization. The review of the literature suggested integrating innovative social finance within the social enterprise business model to ensure financial sustainability through the business model change process. Overall, no previous studies have directly evaluated the social enterprise business model with a specific focus on cash waqf towards affordable healthcare services in India, according to the critical analysis of the literature. As a result, the literature review demonstrates the originality of the current study. The next chapter discusses the journey to explore the effectiveness of endowment in healthcare by describing the research design and methodology utilized to investigate the main research question and objectives.

5

THE JOURNEY TO EXPLORE THE EFFECTIVENESS OF ENDOWMENT IN HEALTHCARE

Apart from non-profit organizations, social enterprises also act as a new alternative method to deliver affordable healthcare. Social enterprises are institutions with social missions whose profits are reinvested in goals that have proven to be a potentially innovative and sustainable solution to accessible healthcare. In order to deliver their healthcare services, social enterprises rely heavily on financial support from governments, corporations, philanthropy, and other donations. However, these sources are diminishing due to the continuing effects of the global financial crisis, decreasing philanthropic giving index, and the instability of some areas of the economy, such as unemployment and corporate profit. According to a recent study, social enterprises encounter obstacles in obtaining appropriate social finance, particularly during the expansion stages of their development.[1] Therefore, one of the most substantial challenges facing social enterprises is how to achieve financial sustainability such that healthcare projects can be managed and sustained over long periods of time. Hence, social enterprises need to explore more community-based philanthropy and diversified sources of funding such as venture philanthropy, philanthrocapitalism, development impact bonds, and endowment investing as pathways to financial sustainability.

Motivation behind the Research

There are a number of studies that have discussed the usage of shariah-based endowments for enterprise funding.[2] An innovative form of waqf, known as cash waqf, is proven to be a successful social finance instrument to fund social enterprises. However, social enterprises fail to secure shariah-based endowment funding because they don't meet social investor's revenue and financial return criteria, or their business model needs to be refined in building sustainable enterprises before they can be considered "investor-ready". Furthermore, to increase access to affordable healthcare and ensure a healthier population, new business models of delivery of healthcare are needed. As a response to these challenges, social enterprises have recently begun to adopt business models that seek to combine financial sustainability through an alternate source of waqf funding. In addition, waqf is well-conceptualized in terms of business model, social enterprise, and social finance, but workable business models of waqf-based social enterprise have yet to be developed and implemented. Hence, more work is required on financing social enterprises through waqf investment to achieve financial sustainability, and more empirical-based research is needed in order to create business models of social enterprise that can provide affordable healthcare services.

The financial sustainability of the social enterprise through waqf-based capital funding is yet to be explored. There is limited research about the healthcare business model of social enterprise with cash waqf funding. A recent study attempted to address the financing of social enterprise through cash waqf in generating capital revenue.[3] The money which a social enterprise receives and uses to deliver its services for profit is referred to as capital revenue. However, the study is limited because the waqf business model is developed specifically for generating capital revenue to invest the cash waqf in other permissible businesses. Moreover, the authors of the same study proposed that further research should be conducted to finance social enterprise through cash waqf in the healthcare sector.

Accordingly, this chapter intends to fill this gap by developing a healthcare business model of social enterprise through cash waqf capital funding. Three bodies of literature are reviewed, namely social enterprises, financial sustainability of social enterprises, and shariah-based endowment investment. Through an analysis of the literature, the context of various researchers' perspectives is examined and concluded by pinpointing the main observations, inconsistencies, and gaps in the field of study relating to the scope of this research.

Since the author of this book is a social entrepreneur in the healthcare sector, it motivated him to delve deeper into this subject. A study was conducted during the COVID-19 crisis, which tremendously challenged the healthcare system and amplified the struggle of social enterprises for financial sustainability. On the other hand, the government of India proposed a social stock exchange in July 2019 to help social enterprises raise capital through equity listing. This encouraged the author/researcher to develop a personal interest in investigating the role of cash waqf in funding the social enterprise business model to provide affordable healthcare services in India. It is with this desire to thoroughly investigate the problem of financial sustainability of social enterprise, the author embarked on a research journey. Figure 1 attempts to capture the author's research journey.

The Main Approach of the Research

A literature review is a critical examination of previous studies that identifies a gap in knowledge in order to justify performing further research. It is the most fundamental and important step in every research project. It is the first step that allows the researcher to become acquainted with potential problems, gain familiarity with field expertise, and define the rationales that drive their research. Despite the fact that there are several review typologies, five distinct broad review methods have been recognized: a systematic literature review, scoping study review, a narrative literature review, a meta-analysis, and a meta-synthesis.

Systematic literature reviews involve gathering, analyzing, and evaluating high-quality literature to establish a solid foundation for a topic and research methodology, particularly common in natural sciences. These reviews aim to test theories, known for their replicable and rigorous design, focusing on a single area with an emphasis on efficacy. On the other hand, scoping study literature reviews identify a broader range of methodological methods, offering a general update on available knowledge and providing an organized framework.

A narrative literature review is a conventional way of examining existing literature, summarizing and synthesizing specific perspectives without aiming for generalization. Despite criticisms for potential subjectivity in selection, narrative reviews are valuable in compiling and synthesizing a large body of literature in specific topic areas, inspiring research ideas and building theory in the humanities and social sciences. However, meta-analysis and meta-synthesis, which involve collective data analysis and conclusions from multiple studies, are not deemed appropriate for this research, as it does not analyze primary data but focuses on the narrative literature review as the most suitable approach to identify gaps and inconsistencies in existing knowledge, determine research questions, and acquire relevant information from diverse sources.

The narrative literature review is sought to identify all that has been written about problems being faced in the health system in India and the role of social enterprise in the sustainable healthcare system in the country. In recent years, there has been a surge in global interest in social enterprise, fueled by a greater understanding of the role social enterprise can play in addressing healthcare concerns. However, lack of access to financing is one of the major impediments to the expansion of the social enterprise sector in India and around the world. Hence, it is crucial to understand the necessity for various sources of finance and how they suit the realities of social enterprises in their pursuit of a long-term social mission. New sources of finance for social enterprises have emerged as a result of recent developments in social investment instruments. This new source of finance is funded by social investors looking for opportunities to fund organizations that generate social value while still making a profit. Shariah-based endowment investment is one such alternative finance instrument allowing social enterprises to have access to social finance. However, only a few attempts have been made to assess the Shariah-based endowment investment as a means of social finance to social enterprises. Therefore, the protocol followed in this narrative literature is as follows— (a) to identify the range and diversity of the available literature based on a defined phenomenon (b) to determine gaps that might spawn new research, (c) to report the available literature.

The range of literature is determined to be within a ten-year timeframe. The phenomenon reviewed is a social enterprise in the healthcare sector, and more specifically, the role of social enterprise in the sustainable healthcare system and financing of social enterprises to provide the necessary background for the present study. The review identifies a theoretical gap in the literature that is targeted by this research, specifically the paucity of in-depth studies of the financial sustainability of social enterprises and business models in the healthcare setting.

The research aims to develop a social enterprise by applying the business model concept within the author's healthcare organization with cash waqf in equity capital funding. The study uses the theories of sustainable social enterprise and business model as the theoretical framework to analyze the financial sustainability of social enterprise with cash waqf investment in equity capital funding. The study aims to explore the central question — What explains the investment in equity capital funding to a sustainable social enterprise healthcare business model to be a cash waqf? The following two objectives are formulated to answer the question —- (a) To substantiate the importance of investment in equity capital funding to social enterprise as a factor for financial sustainability. (b) To develop a sustainable business model of healthcare social enterprise based on the Islamic concept of cash waqf investment to provide affordable health services in India.

The research aims to learn more about social phenomena by looking at the participants' subjective experiences, values, beliefs, ethics, and culture. As a result, the research adopted an interpretivist epistemological viewpoint and a subjectivist ontological perspective in this research. The research adopted a qualitative methodology to achieve the aims of the study and articulated through an action research approach. The reason for the selection of qualitative research design and method is that this study is interested in finding meaning through observations and interviews, and events under complex settings of organizational change that are difficult to achieve through quantitative studies.

The inductive approach of the qualitative study is used for this research since the ultimate aim is to develop a conceptual model based on the research data. Inductive nature is also particularly appropriate for this study since the purpose is to explore the validity of the theories developed through action research. This research focuses on the implementation of the business model within the researcher's healthcare organization. The research is about change within an organization and therefore, an action research approach seems to be the most appropriate and efficient one. This overcomes the practical challenges of studying social enterprises, which is related to the limited opportunity to conduct empirical research. A four-step action research method is used, in which the cycle of "diagnosis", "planning", "taking action", and "assessment of action" is continued until the desired outcome is attained. This method allows the researcher to obtain "real", "solid", and "deep" information that is considered significant, appropriate, and essential to this type of research. Furthermore, purposive sampling is used to conduct face-to-face semi-structured interviews with social investors. These are institutional investors from the financial institutions, foundations, high-net-worth individuals, and individual impact investors. The purpose of the interviews is to examine how social investors perceive cash waqf investment for equity capital funding, what motivates them to consider investing in social enterprise, and the extent of their commitment to support the financial sustainability of the social enterprise.

Philosophy of the Research

The author's philosophical viewpoint steers the research in a specific direction and explains the reasoning behind the research strategy, methodology, design, and methods. A research philosophy encompasses how knowledge is created as well as the characteristics of that knowledge. It reflects how a researcher's knowledge is applied in the study and how their own research approaches, strategies, and methods are utilized. The necessity to obtain a philosophical perspective for any research and an inquiry direction is confirmed in literature too. Therefore, it is mandatory to consider two major approaches to research philosophy— Ontology and Epistemology. Ontology deals with the researcher's assumptions about how the world functions. It emphasizes the nature of reality and is divided into two parts: objectivism and subjectivism. Subjectivism asserts that social phenomena are in actuality formed by social actors concerned with their existence, whereas objectivism asserts that social phenomena exist in reality independent of social actors in relation to their existence. Epistemology is the theory of knowledge that establishes a philosophical foundation for determining what types of knowledge are conceivable and how they are adequate and legitimate. Furthermore, the chosen philosophical approach facilitates a variety of ontology and epistemology-related research paradigms in the social sciences. The significance of analyzing and selecting a philosophy, stems from the fact that it improves the researcher's approach to studying a specific field of action.

Figure 1. The research journey

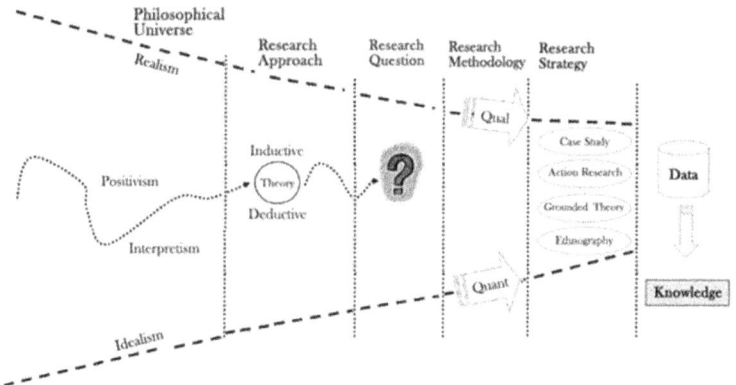

This research falls within the broad field of interest of financial sustainability of social enterprises and the role of cash waqf investment. It is centrally concerned with human thought, feeling, and perception as they relate to the concept of social enterprises. These are challenging and individualized cognitive phenomena that are influenced by a variety of factors, including belief, as well as the attitudes and experiences of social investors and social enterprise owners. While the study in this area could be done, it appeared more constructive to look into the experiences and opinions of present social investors and social enterprises on the subject. Therefore, the required knowledge was gathered in this study by an investigation of the healthcare setting in the Indian context in which social enterprises in need of social financing operate, as well as information obtained from semi-structured interviews. As a result, subjective evidence is compiled based on individual perspectives. This is how knowledge is gained in this study – through people's subjective experiences.

Regarding philosophical concepts, interpretivism and positivism are two popular research paradigms. The aim of interpretive research is to get a better understanding of the phenomena and add depth. Interpretive researchers are primarily interested in investigating specific phenomena. This can be accomplished by employing semi-structured interviews to generate evidence, which leads to a better knowledge of the phenomena in question and answers research questions. Usually, it is supported by the analysis of documentation generated by the case social enterprise involved. It aims to expand the understanding of the phenomena under investigation by examining the perspectives and experiences of the social investors concerning financing for healthcare social enterprise in India. This places the study, which uses qualitative data in the epistemological domain of interpretivism.

This research's ontology, philosophy of knowledge, is relativism: there is no one reality but constructed realities. The epistemology theory of how knowledge is obtained is subjectivist because discoveries are made in the minds of individuals, both as participants and as a whole group. It is critical to demonstrate the research approach as a strategy for improving the validity of social studies. Not only that, but it is also imperative to determine the research approach for three main reasons— Firstly, it aids in answering the research questions by categorizing the types of evidence that must be collected, as well as where and how it must be managed. Secondly, in terms of establishing the research method, an inductive approach is more suitable for understanding rather than describing the phenomena. Lastly, in terms of modifying the research to account for limitations. When conducting research, there are two basic approaches to consider— Inductive and Deductive. Within a study, a researcher can employ these approaches separately or in tandem. Deductive research begins with a hypothesis and then tests hypotheses generated from the theory. In this approach, a theory has usually been developed before data collection. For this study, choosing a deductive approach for practical studies provides several obstacles:

1. The study must identify a contemporary, relevant, and fascinating theory that is sufficiently specific to allow the formation and testing of hypotheses.
2. It must devise practical and reliable measures of critical

variables, as well as appropriate controls.
3. Due to its rigid structure, the deductive approach would prevent the researcher from delving deeply into the concerns, limiting the ability to evaluate the occurrences under investigation.

In the inductive approach, researchers collect data and generate a theory as a theoretical model for the outcome of their data analysis. In this approach, an idea has been developed after the collection of data. This development is achieved by analyzing the research data, which leads to new insight into different entities and an understanding of the nature of the research subject. In contrast to the deductive approach, an inductive research approach uses qualitative data and diverse data collection methods to efficiently explore different views of phenomena. It also requires a small sample of research subjects as it deals with contexts and events that have already occurred. Hence, the inductive approach is generally associated with the qualitative research design. For several factors, this research study is better suited to an inductive rather than a deductive one. First of all, the study will aid in developing theory, adding new insights, and closing the research gap in financial sustainability, social enterprise business model, and cash waqf. Moving on, subjectivism philosophies align with creating an understanding of the views and feelings of social enterprise owners in India's healthcare establishment and social investors. Apart from this, the study is interested in something other than deducing hypotheses, testing hypotheses in practice, or expressing hypotheses in operational terms.

Methodology of the Research

In order to fulfill the aim of the research and its objectives, researchers need to link their philosophy, approach, and methods with actual practice. This can be done by choosing the proper research methodology, data collection, and data analysis procedures. Hence, the decision to adopt a particular research methodology is mainly influenced by the research subject, objectives, existing knowledge, research philosophy, resources, and time frame. The research methodology is the overall path that the research takes, often divided into quantitative and qualitative.

The quantitative research method was originally developed to investigate natural phenomena. It is more objective in nature and typically supports positivism philosophy. It usually seeks to discover the cause & effect relationships between variables in a phenomenon. In addition, it essentially uses a deductive approach by focusing on collecting numerical data, measuring phenomena, and analyzing statistics to explore the hypothetical model. Despite the difficulty in its initial design, this research method is highly structured, and can be easily presented statistically. However, during data collection and analysis, this systematic structure would be considered as the most evident drawback of this method; because it can limit the exploration of other areas and prevent researchers from making new data.

The term qualitative is concerned with the qualities of entities, processes, and meanings that are not statistically examined. Therefore, when data analysis is based on interpretations of words rather than numbers, the form of research method for answering research inquiries is termed qualitative. The qualitative research method explores and understands the meaning individuals or groups ascribe to a social or human problem. As a field of inquiry, this method can crosscut diverse disciplines based on complex, interrelated sets of concepts. It consists of various interpretations that make the world visible and turns it into groups of representations. For e.g., interviews, field notes, and photographs. These interpretations refer to carving a sense of phenomena in terms of the meanings people give to them within a particular natural setting. Thus, the qualitative research method focuses on exploring data, uncovering particularities of the phenomena, and describing findings based on the context of the study.

Instead of focusing on the frequency of social events, qualitative research frequently aims to identify and characterize them in detail and investigate why they occur. The nature of the research question in this study suggests the qualitative methodology. The question is not worded as "how many" and the emphasis is not on testing or verification; instead, the goal is for respondents to understand the situation better and develop a new model. Furthermore, the drawbacks of the quantitative method can negatively affect the aim and objectives of this research project. As a result, employing a qualitative research methodology will aid in exploring and identifying the significant issues and challenges in the research setting, as indicated in the meanings expressed by the respondent's words.

In general, a methodology for any research provides legitimacy and scientifically sound data. The research methodology of healthcare aims to understand societal phenomena by scrutinizing the participant's subjective experiences, values, beliefs, ethics, and culture. The author's research adopted a qualitative methodology to achieve the aims of the study. Since this study is interested in exploring meaning through observations, interviews, and events under complex settings of organizational changes that are difficult to achieve through quantitative analyses, a qualitative research design has been adopted.

Design of the Research

The overall research plan for researchers to collect and analyze data, respond to research inquiries, meet research aims and objectives, and address research limits and ethical considerations has been described as research design. It refers to a procedure of study that includes everything from the underlying worldviews to the specific research methods. As a result, the nature of the research subject, philosophical assumptions, interests and experiences of researchers, research strategy, data collecting, analysis, and interpretation influence the decision to use a given research design. The goal of adopting qualitative research methodology is to understand a particular phenomenon from the perspective and behavior of those who are experiencing the phenomenon. Several qualitative research methods include grounded theory, case study, ethnography, action research, narrative, historical studies, conversational analysis, discourse analysis, ethnomethodology, and phenomenology. The techniques and procedures used to collect data and fulfill the research aim and objectives are referred to as research methods. Phenomenology, grounded theory, and ethnography are more commonly used qualitative approaches in healthcare. Ethnography, grounded theory, and action research methods are used to provide fresh insights into the entrepreneurship field. In order to study the business model, innovation, case study, and action research methods have been used. Since the current research area covers healthcare, entrepreneurship, and business model innovation, ethnography, grounded theory, phenomenology, case study, and action research methods, they shall be examined. The research methods explored in this context are the following:

Ethnographic research describes and interprets the shared and learned patterns of values, behaviors, beliefs, and language of the group. The method involves extended observations through participant observation, in which the researcher is immersed in the people's day-to-day lives, observes, and interviews the group participants related to health and illness. In healthcare, it has been used in topics related to health beliefs and practices, allowing these issues to be viewed in the context in which they occur and, therefore, helping broaden the understanding of behaviors related to healthcare and illness. However, ethnography can infringe on the rights and privacy of the patients. Furthermore, this needs to have knowledge of the past and cultures of patients in healthcare and customers in entrepreneurship. Therefore, ethnography is not considered for this research.

Grounded theory is a mid-range method that focuses on the process and connects different stages of theory. It focuses on familiar experiences to provide an explanation or theory behind the events. It has the benefit of generating innovative business concepts. It also offers the appropriate inquiry processes to address research issues at the micro-level of social entrepreneurial activity. However, grounded theory is limited— it lacks reproducibility and generalizability across healthcare social enterprises. Furthermore, the process of abstracting and encompassing new business concepts and categories is tiring and laborious in grounded theory. The case study method is defined as "the study of a case within a real-life contemporary context or setting." It is an approach to studying, discovering underlying problems, and explaining an organization, entity, company, or event. Case studies are bound explicitly by time and space constraints to discover information about real-life versus theoretical issues. The case studies research can be explanatory, exploratory, or descriptive. Researchers argue that a case study is a suitable approach when the objective is to understand a contemporary phenomenon whose boundaries from the real-life context need to be more evident. The case study method is widely used in exploring business model design, entrepreneurial ventures, and business model innovation. However, it is also biased in data collection, internal or outside the organization, and can result in improper results.

As mentioned previously, the action research method is an approach in which the action researcher collaborates with diagnosing the problem and developing a solution based on the diagnosis. In this research method, researchers and members of the organization join hands to solve the organization's situation. It is a participatory study consisting of a spiral of self-reflective cycles with planning, acting, observing, and reflecting. It represents a potentially powerful research method to be adopted within social entrepreneurship. As the business model innovation is understood through changes in the organizations by taking actions, the concept of action research is well-aligned with the idea of business model innovation and social enterprise. This research focuses on implementing the business model within the researcher's healthcare organization. The research is about change within an organization. Thus, an action research approach seems to be the most appropriate for this study.

Interviews are the most popular methods for gathering information about any research. There are three kinds of interviews: structured, semi-structured, and unstructured, defined as organized, informed, and guided in a few books, respectively. The semi-structured interview is used more often in qualitative research in health care. It is based on a dynamic subject guide that offers a loose framework of open-ended questions to discuss perceptions and attitudes. It has the benefit of great flexibility, allowing the researcher to enter new areas and generate more information. However, this method has a limitation— the information gathered from interviews is based on what people say rather than what they do. This may result in discrepancies between the interviewee's assertion and their actual behavior. The goal is to get their thoughts and comments on how to fund social enterprises in India with cash waqf through capital equity funding. Semi-structured interviews allow the researcher to go deeper into a subject in order to elicit additional information from the interviewee. It also gives an in-depth examination of the perceptions of distinct groups, which offers diverse perspectives on social enterprises.

Research sampling and data analysis

Sampling strategies are primarily determined by the study's purpose in qualitative research. In this research, sampling aims to classify specific groups of people with characteristics or live in the circumstances similar to the phenomenon being studied. It allows established informants to explore attitudes and behavioral aspects related to the research. Sampling techniques are a set of strategies that enables the researcher to diminish the amount of data required by considering data from a subset of cases rather than all possible elements. Generally, there are two essential sampling types- probability sampling and non-probability sampling.

When the size of the population is known, and a sample is ordinarily equal in all circumstances, probability sampling or representative sampling is utilized. This form of selection necessitates the researcher to approximate the population's attributes statistically from the sample. It's usually related to surveys and experimental research methods. Non-probability sampling encompasses a variety of ways for picking samples depending on the researcher's judgment. The probability of each case is normally chosen from an unknown population in this form of sampling. To answer research questions and fulfill the research aim, the researcher must make statistical inferences about the population's characteristics. In the present research, a non-probability sampling technique is used with a purposive sampling strategy to select the study elements. Since qualitative research is undertaken to gain a deeper understanding of phenomena, the researcher chose a small sample, i.e., capital equity funding in one healthcare social enterprise within a specific context of India.

Data analysis is described as interpretation, making sense of data, or transforming data. The analysis is sometimes interpreted to suggest different language, theory, or interpretive/descriptive research procedures. However, there may be similarities between these different methods, and a researcher may choose to use a language-based method of analysis, such as a symbolic interactionist, while at the same time developing a theory. The case of the research is analyzed using the coding process where first-level raw data is converted into concepts followed by grouping the similar concepts into a higher level of abstraction called subcategories and categories. The transcribed interviews and documents are coded with respect to the main categories of interest, their properties, and their dimensions. Coding describes the analytical process through which data are conceptualized and integrated into theoretical statements, models, or frameworks.

Ethics can be defined as the norms for conduct that distinguish between acceptable and unacceptable behavior. Given the significance of ethics for the conduct of research, many different professional associations and universities have adopted specific guidelines, rules, and policies relating to research ethics. Ethics in research relies on considerations such as not breaching confidentiality, not distorting data, informed consent, honesty, and the right to withdraw. Ethical considerations involved in the research design include examining issues associated with perceived bias and coercion. Action research is a unique and complex approach to research. The relationship between the researcher and participants collaborating in an action research study gives rise to ethical dilemmas relating to selection and voluntary participation, informed consent, decision-making, anonymity and confidentiality, conflicting and different needs, and data interpretation. Ethical issues in action research are inherently linked to role duality. Existing roles and relationships of the individual researcher, participants/co-researchers, and internal and external stakeholders comprise the arena in which ethical issues are played out.

The overall research methodology and the justification for using a qualitative research design to investigate the research question have been described thoroughly. The qualitative research enabled a better understanding of a complex subject: how innovative social finance is integrated into a social enterprise's business model and the financial sustainability it achieves. Considering that health systems are evolving rapidly, the economic sustainability issues associated with social enterprises are becoming increasingly challenging. As a result, the exploratory nature of qualitative research adopting an inductive approach was beneficial in this study since it facilitated the discovery of new aspects of business model innovation in a social enterprise. As already stated, the inductive approach of the qualitative study has been used in this research since the ultimate aim is to develop a conceptual model based on the research data. An inductive nature is particularly appropriate for this study since the purpose is to explore the validity of the theories developed through action research. It focuses on implementing the business model within the researcher's healthcare organization. Since it is about change within an organization, an action research approach is the most appropriate. It overcomes the practical challenges of studying social enterprises related to the limited opportunity to conduct empirical research. In this study, a four-step action research method is used- The cycle of diagnosis, planning, taking action, and assessment of action is continued until the desired outcome is attained.

6

THE SUSTAINABILITY OF THE BUSINESS MODEL

Sustainability as a term has been extensively debated by culture, businesses, and governments in recent years. The sustainability of any organization can be calculated in terms of its effect on the three pillars of sustainable development: social, economic, and environmental influence. Businesses must incorporate sustainable values into their strategies to promote sustainable development. The three dimensions of economic, environmental, and social factors are generally discussed and categorized into the main issues of sustainability— (a) Economic: Value creation, economic performance, profit, financial resilience, and market position are all important factors. (b) Social: Workplace procedures, working conditions, diversity, equal opportunity, adherence to social policies, well-being, community development, health and safety, livelihood, and human rights are all things to consider. (c) Environmental: Flows of energy and resources, pollution prevention, waste, transportation, and the coexistence of humans and nature.

One of the major problems surrounding the issue of measuring social enterprise success and sustainability is the creation of performance indicators. Examples of such measures include performance indicators using Statistical Process Control. However, these performance indicators focus on patient safety culture and satisfaction and not the sustainability of the organization. Sustainable development goals (SDG) and composite indicators are thought to be useful tools for measuring sustainable development and its progress. The Global Reporting Initiative (GRI) is one of the most widely disseminated proposals for sustainability indicators, which studies the indicators collection that appears in an organization's sustainability study.[1] However, there are no globally agreed-upon benchmarks for the sustainability of social enterprise that could be used to monitor progress. Moreover, the literature on sustainability indicators has one thing in common— it recognizes that an organization's sustainability is multi-dimensional and interdependent.

Furthermore, considering the specific focus of social enterprises on achieving financial sustainability, the financial results must be measured. Thus, leading to the introduction of the key performance indicators (KPIs). A model that defined a set of KPIs proposed a multidimensional control system that constructed a map of indicators to measure social enterprise performance.[2] Financial performance, social effectiveness, and institutional legitimacy are the three performance dimensions stated in the model. In particular, financial performance is defined in terms of revenue, cash flows, and cost of services. These KPIs are essential that reflect the financial performance of the social enterprise in the healthcare segment.

As social enterprise research expands on several fronts, it has been comprehensible that social enterprises are multidimensional in nature and require a multidisciplinary approach when studying the literature. The commercial operation to collect financial resources and social goals mainly associated with a social mission and objectives are defined as the two main distinguishing characteristics of social enterprises. The business model construct is indirectly linked in the literature on social enterprise to the organization's ability to be financially sustainable, which is based on revenue-generating activities. The business model is described as a cost and revenue architecture that explains how an organization generates value by delivering unique healthcare services to individual paying customers and captures value through earned income. Hence, both practitioners and academics agree that social enterprise organizations need to adapt business models in order to ensure sustainability, especially financial sustainability.[3]

The principle of the business model for sustainability has gained attention in the past few years. There is no universally agreed definition of the business model for sustainability, just as there is no universally accepted definition of business models. This definition is described as a model that generates competitive advantage by providing superior customer value while also contributing to the long-term growth of businesses and society. It encompasses programs that address social and/or environmental issues. It has a good market impact by doing so. All of them deal with consumer and social value generation, as well as the convergence of social, environmental, and economic activities. Economic principles are often the subject of traditional business models. Furthermore, the business model for sustainability needs the incorporation of additional sustainable perspectives. Although the economic perspective is already discussed in various sectors, there are additional factors to consider when designing a sustainable business. Only a few studies have attempted to conceptualize the elements of sustainable businesses and their relationships. There is a study that recognizes ideal types of business models for sustainability, analyzes the possible business model for sustainability in the context of industry. It also distinguishes archetypes of the business model for sustainability, examines the influence of archetypes like product-service-systems, presents case studies, and develops methodologies for innovation.

Business models are often perceived as a collaborative innovation for sustainable value development. In literature, the definition of 'value' underpins the concept of a business model. It has a direct relation to the realization of economic value, the interlocking elements that generate and produce value, and the support of the customer's value proposition among other items. A firm's value development logic accepts the incorporation of social objectives into a more holistic sense of value from a sustainability standpoint. A major driver of social enterprise is the production of social capital in addition to economic value. The figure below illustrates a conceptual framework for sustainable value that incorporates economic, environmental, and social values:

Figure 1: Conceptual Framework of Sustainability

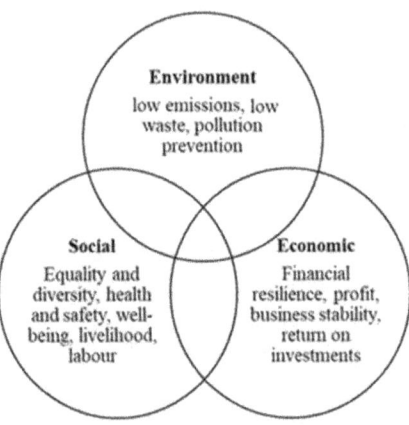

Since the business model is a value creation process, the issue of how to determine the business model's sustainability arises. It is critical to assess the principles in business model frameworks that discuss sustainability in order to determine which approaches can be integrated, which can be used in specific domains, and which can facilitate the efficient construction of these models. A general framework is required due to the diversity of current methods. As a result, a preliminary assessment of the following factors is recommended:[4]

(a) Evaluation inside the single type of typology: Firstly, it is suggested to evaluate the possibilities of combining aspects from a single typology category. Is it possible to merge all of the aspects, or does one aspect obstruct the others? Is it true that applying a view to a single building block precludes adding a view to the entire business model? These questions should be considered.

(b) Evaluation between all types of the typology: Secondly, compare and contrast the different methods. Is it possible to merge different approaches? For example, is it possible to add new boxes while also changing the content of existing boxes? Is it permissible to integrate sustainability evaluations by using a domain-specific modeling technique? To answer these questions, it needs a mix of each kind. It must be examined how each form interacts with the others to answer these questions.

(c) Evaluation of domain-specific applicability: Thirdly, assess the typology forms' applicability to determine which domains/use cases they are appropriate for. In what situations does it make sense to choose a particular type? For example, in social business models, splitting the revenue stream into blocks based on financial and social benefits is very common.

The results of an assessment may show that the existing methods are perfectly adequate for modeling sustainable businesses and that no further improvements are needed. Since current enhancements are difficult to understand and use, changing the business model is one of the best ways to consider sustainability. There is a business model development and business model interpretation viewpoint that focuses on the performance and effectiveness of sustainability in general. The sustainability of the business model is assessed using indicators or metrics to determine how sustainable a business model is. When the sustainability of social enterprises is assessed, the social mission is located at the core of the organization. For this reason, social enterprises' specific social aims are considered before constituting a business model. Therefore, social entrepreneurs have to seek innovative business models that place their organizations' social mission at the core of achieving sustainability.[5]

Business Model Innovation for Sustainable Development

For sustainable development, business model innovation is mandatory.[6] The innovation process provides new combinations of resources, tools, and the business models have a role in identifying the way healthcare service providers present their beneficiaries with the value proposition and create and capture the economic value. In this way, business model development consists of handling the innovation cycle, how the healthcare provider works together with all stakeholders, i.e., how the organization develops, performs, and values. The development in healthcare business models can have different motivations as a starting point: Having a (reactive) problem with them; modifying, developing or defending existing models to adapt them to a changing (adaptive) environment; bringing new (expansive) technology, goods or services onto the market; preparing for the future, researching and evaluating entirely new business models that may eventually replace existing ones (proactive/exploratory). Researchers have studied how a business model can be innovative with a change of a component. The focus of the research is on the *types* of business model innovation. There are three types of business model innovation that can be integrated: (a) Revenue model innovation – the way a healthcare establishment generates revenue. (b) Enterprise model innovation– changing the internal structure of the healthcare establishment. (c) Industry model innovation – redefining existing industries or creating a new industry. Business model innovation for sustainability is defined as the creation of novel forms of exchange at some point along a company's value chain that enables a business to respect environmental limits while fulfilling social wants and needs. In certain studies by Boons, F., & Lüdeke-Freund, the practice of sustainability practices in organizations is associated with the term innovation that is always identical with the use of technology in order to create a low ecological impact of products and services. However, business model innovation for sustainability is also defined as innovations that create significant positive or significantly reduced negative impacts for the society through changes in the way the organization delivers and captures value.

Furthermore, the concept of sustainability is found associated with the innovative financing methods of the business.[7] Financing for social enterprise can be innovative, including equity, debt, grants, donation, and public funding. Innovative financing structures may be built even within conventional means, depending on the desired outcomes. Innovative financing is also commonly thought to have a risk-distribution aspect, in which risk is distributed over a large number of investors and guaranteed by higher-rated third parties. The definition encompasses strategies for bridging the capital gap by recasting successful financial instruments that are understood by the healthcare sector in a way that supports sustainable business development. The thoughtful use of financial instruments and strategies to enable capital to attain a social, environmental, and financial return is termed social finance. Unlike traditional financing methods that require a trade-off between financial return and social impact, social finance is a long-term money management strategy that gives social, environmental, and economic benefits. This innovative social financing is reflected in increased earned income streams in the healthcare sector, ensuring the sustainability of the social enterprise business model.

Integrating Sustainability into a Business Model of Social Enterprise

The pursuit of financial and social sustainability at the same time is quickly becoming a strategic goal for businesses in all sectors and regions. Also, businesses that have put considerable resources and effort into incorporating sustainability into their business models are finding it increasingly difficult to handle the learning and transformation processes required to address the social problem due to a lack of clarity in the factors and change processes that influence an organization's ability to adapt to sustainability. Simultaneously, management researchers are working to establish conceptual frameworks and empirical evidence for these particularly complex evolutionary processes. A sustainable business model was developed to integrate sustainability into an organization's decision-making process as well as influence the organization's social goal.[8] A framework for integrating sustainability into a business model was proposed as a part of the process of devising strategies for developing and changing the business models.[9] The framework devised a set of measures that could transform conventional business models in order to address societal sustainability. Another researcher attempted to conceptualize a sustainable business model by creating a structure that integrates sustainability techniques and innovation by taking into account both the private and public sectors.[10]

Integrating sustainability into an organization's business model necessitates that, in addition to economic stakeholders, society be addressed as well. The value captured for the organization and its major stakeholders, such as society, is the subject of a business model. A business model that includes society as part of the range of stakeholders can be a catalyst for achieving sustainability. Since the business model definition in the literature is captured in terms of value creation and value capture, a business model may serve as a connection between the value generated and captured and the value recipients. Sustainable business models capture economic and social value for a broad range of stakeholders. However, in order to generate and distribute value to customers, an organization must be able to change business models. As a result, an organization's business model must change in order to generate total value for all of the organization's stakeholders.

As already mentioned above, there are two key discussions in the literature about business model change— The first focuses on the creation of new business models & the second topic of discussion is the change of existing business models. Well, organizational change processes related to evolving business models are referred to as business model change. This study belongs to the latter part of the discussion. The literature on the business model change as organizational change examines a variety of modes of change, ranging from basic replication of current business models to gradual change such as renewal, rebuilding, revision, expansion, and evolution, as well as more dramatic modes of change such as re-invention, restructuring, or termination of a business model.[11] Business model change is also explained as emergent in and within business model components, according to a relational interpretation. Since a business model is made up of so many diverse components, it is helpful to figure out which ones are foundational. Identifying foundational business model components can help with future business model change analysis.

The various business model components can be used to track the development of business model frameworks. These business model frameworks are primarily focused on the frequency with which certain components appear, as well as the context of certain components, value proposition, customer segment, revenue, key resources, key partners, key activities, and related components. Some of these components, however, may be defined as sub-dimensions of other components in some cases. The value and financial model themes are described as the two key themes in general. The value theme encompasses all aspects of value offering, value capture, and value formation, while the financial theme encompasses all aspects of financial planning and control in a business model. The financial model theme was the second key theme that is established from the business model components. Financial planning and control through a free flow of capital, as well as cost structure analysis, necessitate a well-structured financial model. There are six dimensions to the financial model of the business model framework. Models include the financing model, revenue model, price model, expense model, profit model, and delivery model. The financing model highlights the money sources required to carry out the business model. The equity capital of the business model is financed through social financing. As a capital component of the social enterprise business model, social finance aids the organization's financial sustainability. Cash waqf is an innovative form of waqf, which has proved to be a successful social finance instrument for funding social enterprises.

Identification of Financial Sustainability Elements for the Model Acceptability

The ability of an organization to endure over time is referred to as sustainability. In the context of social enterprise, there are two sides to sustainability. One side is concerned with an organization's ability to survive and thrive financially over time. The other side does not seem obvious to assess financial endurance without considering whether an organization's social mission can continue, retain or deepen its influence over time. However, by separating the social impact and financial outcomes, the best chance of creating sustainable social enterprises can be ensured. Identifying and analyzing the elements of financial performance indicators is important for developing measures to ensure the financial sustainability of the social enterprise and is the key factor in accepting the proposed conceptual model.

In general, researchers write on balance between several components while analyzing a social enterprise's financial sustainability. According to the literature, revenue and expenses along with assets and liabilities must be balanced to assess the financial sustainability of the organization.[12] Many researchers look at it from this perspective by focusing on bookkeeping and how assets, liabilities, income, and spending are balanced.[13] However, this approach does not allow for the analysis of financial sustainability as a complex of financial and non-financial aspects. In order to assess a system of financial sustainability, it is necessary to identify the financial performance dimension of key performance indicators.

The key performance indicators include indicators for organizational, market, operational, and financial sustainability. The indicator describes the enterprise's current state and chances for enhancing its quality of operation. The following characteristics of an enterprise make up the system of financial sustainability indicators: product/service quality, company management quality, financial state of the company, and operating indicators risks. The core element of the represented system is that of financial condition indicators. Financial condition is not only a notion in traditional financial analysis but also a tool for sustainable development in other areas of enterprise, such as social sustainability.

Parallelly, financial statements have been considered to be a valuable tool for determining the financial sustainability of enterprises. According to the International Federation of Accountants (IFAC), the Income Statement is a useful tool for assessing financial sustainability due to its strong link to the equity concept, which is considered to be the most important condition because it considers future generations. As a result, the Income Statement becomes a critical tool with two purposes: (a) to determine the social enterprise's capacity to continue providing at least the same level of social impacts (b) to determine the financial resources which will be required to meet its future service delivery obligations. This study will use the gross profit and share capital indicators of the financial statement of the social enterprise to assess the financial sustainability of the organization. Now that we have identified the elements required for financial sustainability, it is important to delve into the healthcare business model of the social enterprise with cash waqf investment.

Healthcare Business Model of the Social Enterprise with Cash Waqf Investment

A conceptual study allows the researcher to build artifacts as well as generate a completely new way of looking at an issue, making it more than just a literature review. It primarily consists of a creative design of framework as well as a synthesis, which distinguishes it from a literature review. In response to the identified knowledge gap, this chapter presents the theoretical development of social enterprise through the business model innovation process found in the literature and synthesizes them into a conceptual framework. The conceptual connection between business model and innovative financing for the sustainability of the social enterprise in this study is made through the business model change process resulting in a new business model innovation framework. This framework is the basis for the empirical investigations to answer the research question.

Therefore, the author attempted to propose a conceptual framework based on the above studies in the field of sustainability of the social enterprise, business models of social enterprise, and attaining the financial sustainability of the social enterprise through the business model change. The proposed conceptual framework was predominantly informed by the work on financing social enterprises through cash waqf– an innovation of business model by Mohd. Zain in the year 2021. The work was done by a team led by Mohd. Zain. His team members consisted of Nor Razinah, Nur Fauziah, Najim, Zakariyah, Habeebullah, Mohd. Noor, Azman, and of course, Mohd. Zain respectively. According to the study, cash waqf can be used to generate capital revenue for social enterprises if the required principles of cash waqf as stipulated by Islamic law are met. According to Islamic law, cash waqf refers to a founder's commitment to a sum of money and the dedication of its usufruct in perpetuity to prescriptive purposes. Irrevocability, perpetuity, and inalienability are the most significant features of cash waqf that have been agreed upon by most Muslim jurists. They state that the cash waqf must be in perpetuity, as the revenue earned should provide sustainable and continuous support.

Mohd. Zain and his team further proposed a modern business model of social enterprise in combination with the innovative version of religious social finance, i.e., cash waqf, to carry out the operation of social enterprise. However, their study proposed cash waqf investment to a social enterprise which further invests in social business, generating profits. The investments of cash waqf are made with the equity financing contracts for micro-small enterprises. Furthermore, all the proposed models by various studies — Elgari, M.A, The Qard Hassan bank, Cizakca, M. Cash waqf as alternative to Nonbank Financial Institutions (NBFIs) bank, Ahmed, H. Waqf-Based Microfinance, Tohirin, A. The cash waqf for empowering the small businesses, Mohsin, M. I. A. Financing through cash-waqf, Duasa, J. and Thaker have similarities, which is the participation contract between cash waqf institutions and micro-small enterprises. Although the various cash waqf models that have been proposed by various authors have shown the possibility of integrating cash waqf and micro-enterprises to effectively address the issue of financing for micro-enterprises demonstrating the financial sustainability of the organization but does not examine the business model of micro-enterprises.

The aforementioned study does not dwell on business model theory and the development of innovative components in the business model. Secondly, the proposed framework makes assumptions of business in which cash waqf investment is made in a social business. Thirdly, the business model is not designed to guarantee the profit generated from the social business. Therefore, to fill this gap, this research study proposes an innovative business model of a healthcare social enterprise that seeks investment through cash waqf and provides affordable healthcare services. Social enterprises have started benefiting from venture capitalist strategies in order to ensure their financial sustainability. A sustainable model is proposed in the literature to improve the management of cash waqf by employing venture capitalist thought and strategies such as formulating the business strategies, management team, and helping the investor as an enterprise.

The practice of cash waqf investment in social enterprises encouraged the author to come up with a business model innovation of social enterprise that can be developed, not only to generate profit to provide financial sustainability but also to create a social impact whereby underprivileged citizens are served with their healthcare needs. This framework is presented in the form of a conceptual model, shown in Figure 2, in which it is posited that the applicable components of business model in the business activity of the social enterprise through healthcare services and well-being of individuals and communities. While this framework is in a relatively early stage of conceptualization, its approach to building a sustainable business model innovation process through business model change concepts and business model innovation-focused tools is promising because of the advanced literature in these areas. It is intended that this initial conceptualization will be developed and refined through evidence and theory building, informed both by the 'state of the art' of the literature presented in this chapter and also by the results of the empirical phase of this action research study.

The concept was obtained from the existing literature in terms of the conceptual framework. Specifically, business model factors of social enterprise and innovation elements are integrated through business model change into underlying concepts, which can be defined unambiguously and employed in a conceptual model.

Thereafter, the existing knowledge is consolidated through the three change elements (enterprise, industry, and revenue) of business model innovation, attaining financial sustainability. The conceptual model elucidates the mechanisms needed to transform the business model of social enterprise into a sustainable business model that can be obtained from social investment.

Figure 2. Conceptual framework of sustainable social enterprise business model (SSEBM) with cash waqf investment

(Developed by the Author, 2021)

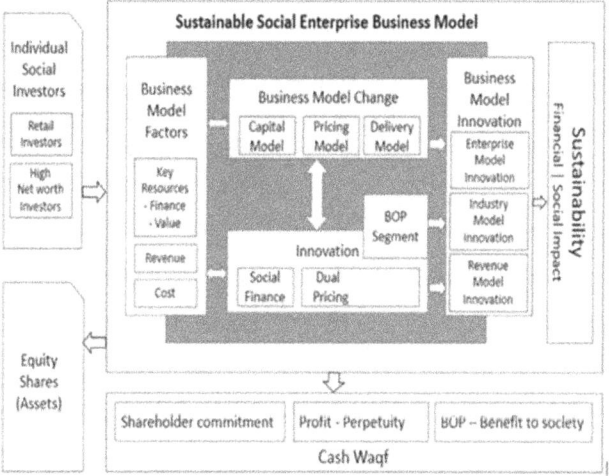

The above diagram demonstrates the proposed conceptual framework for the sustainable social enterprise business model (SSEBM). This model is based on fundraising for the social enterprise using equity-based financing from individuals and communities. The entities used in the model such as business model factors (key resources – finance, value, revenue, and cost), innovation elements (cash waqf social finance, dual pricing, and BOP segment), and the interaction between them through the business model change process to result into business model innovation (enterprise model, industry model, and revenue model) are explained. The model is based on the following assumptions:

(a) Individuals and high net worth individuals make direct payments to social enterprises.
(b) The social enterprise issues the equity shares to the individual against the investment made.
(c) Social enterprise offers healthcare services to self-paying patients at a profit margin and free to BOP.
(d) The profit generated out of self-paying patients is used to fund the healthcare services to BOP.
(e) If there is still a lack of funds, then social investors finance the remaining amount.
(f) There is no distribution of profits from the social enterprise to shareholders according to their share.
(g) At the end of each year, the social enterprise submits the financial report to shareholders.
(h) It is ascertained that risk in investing in social enterprise is unavoidable, just like any other investment. However, to manage risk, a portion of the investment may be invested in assets of the social enterprise.

In the proposed conceptual framework, business model factors representing key resources, revenue, and cost include sub-factors like finance and value proposition. These factors are also referred to as structural factors since they comprise regulations and resources for social enterprise activities, as defined by Anthony Giddens. In other words, these factors govern and supply resources for social enterprise activity. First and foremost, the key resource is a crucial factor for social enterprises because it influences their sustainability by fostering social enterprises, offering value propositions, and providing financial resources. Secondly, cost is one of the most significant factors of the business model for social enterprise, which drives profits. As a result, social enterprises need to choose an appropriate pricing model and diversify it, adapting their innovation and investment strategies. Finally, the importance of the revenue factor in the development of social enterprises must be considered. The impact of the revenue factor on the sustainability of social enterprises may be more significant than other factors.

In economies, the bottom of the pyramid (BOP) is the largest, but poorest socio-economic group. The BOP represents people who are represented in the bottom (4th) tier of the world income pyramid. The more current usage refers to the people living on less than $2 per day, as first defined in 1998 by C.K. Prahlad and Staurt.

L. Hart. C.K. Prahlad has largely highlighted the concept of BOP in his research papers. Four billion people, a majority of the world's population, constitute the base of the economic pyramid. In the year 2007, Prahalad & Landrum had put forward that BOP should be "viewed as a growth opportunity and as a source of innovation" in terms of products, services, business models and so forth within the private sector. As with a more recent trend "the poor are increasingly recognized as highly resourceful entrepreneurs who possess valuable knowledge, resources and capabilities". Prahlad further proposes that business, governments and donor agencies stop-thinking of the poor as victims and instead start seeing them as resilient and creative entrepreneurs as well as value-demanding consumers. The government has been promoting programs such as Financial Inclusion, Unique Identification (UIDAI), Internet and mobile connectivity for the BOP. According to DI International Business Development (DIBD) report, Doing BOP Business in South Africa– March 2010, on their trip to South Africa, to explore the potential for doing business in South Africa, found that in order to sell sustainable products to BOP markets, companies can significantly expand their consumer base and at the same time empower poor people to be lifted out of poverty. The BOP markets rest on low margin per unit and high volume. To successfully manage business conditions at the BOP, the companies must be innovative in their approach and customize their products, production, and prices to the realities in BOP markets.

Business Model Innovation Through Process Change

Innovating an existing business model by modifying the organizational activities and structures regarding BMI impacts the sustainability of the social enterprise. Building upon the insights of the identified business model factors, three innovation elements are outlined for the business model innovation framework. Accounting for these identified business model components, a framework of BMI is presented to deal with the operational details of the nature of the innovation. The framework refers to target customers, value propositions, and delivery systems. These BMI factors are basically for the characteristics of the BMI framework. Innovation through target group changes (including the BOP segment), through value propositions change (free services to BOP), and through value delivery change (changing the pricing model). Therefore, BOP segments are essential for social enterprises for the possible financial benefits and the social impact they create by providing access to new products or services, i.e., value proposition. Concerning the BMI framework, these innovative elements of social finance, dual pricing, and the BOP segment are solid components of the BMI framework that require modification of the business model through the business model change process. The modified business model addresses the degree of sustainability of the resulting business model innovation of social enterprise.

Business model change as organizational change examines a variety of modes of change, ranging from a simple replication of existing business models to incremental change in the forms of renewal, rebuilding, revision, extension, and evolution, as well as more drastic changes such as re-invention, innovation, transformation, or termination of a business model. Adding activities, integrating existing activities, or changing how an activity is done are examples of changes. This conceptual framework outlines disruptive business model change through innovation. Table 1 sets out essential elements of the business model of the conceptual framework, activities, and initiatives in which healthcare social enterprise is involved, and changes in the business model to integrate the innovation elements of the BMI framework. The Giesen model is best suited for changing the business model.[14] Column 1 of Table 1 shows the types of revenue, enterprise, and industry elements of Giesen's business model framework that need to be changed to develop a revised business model. Column 2 of Table 1 shows the previous revenue (standard pricing), enterprise (taxable income), and industry (marketing expense) elements of the social enterprise. Column 3 of Table 1 shows the desired change in the revenue, business, and industrial aspects of the changed business model.

Table 1. Social Enterprise Business Model Change

Business Model Level	Social Enterprise Business Model (Before Business Model Change)	Sustainable Social Enterprise Model (After Business Model Change)
Revenue Business Model Innovation (Economic Level)	One price for all strategies. No fixed and regular income.	Minimum price strategy for patients with BOP. Income from self-paying patients.
Enterprise Business Model Innovation (Operational level)	One product (value proposition) for all. Single delivery model. Grant and Debt financing.	Products and services offering variation. Multiple delivery models. Social equity financing.
Industry Business Model Innovation (Strategic Level)	Free treatment to all patients, including self-paying patients. CSR strategy to serve patients with BOP.	Patients with BOP are included in the patient segment. Profit generation through dual pricing

Innovation in the business model is implemented through a business model change in organizations by taking actions. Therefore, the concept of action research aligns well with the integration of innovation in the business model, especially innovation in healthcare establishments is incremental and relies on experimentation with trial and error to enable healthcare establishments. It fits well with action research, which in turn requires intervention to alter circumstances and implement an innovative business model from those actions. Action research in healthcare is a transformative approach that continuously innovates in healthcare to improve patient experiences and the population's health, reduce healthcare costs, and enhance the experience of healthcare providers. Furthermore, an innovative business model protects and expands the sustainability of the healthcare social enterprise.

Thus, we have learnt from this chapter that a conceptual framework was developed to achieve the financial sustainability of the social enterprise. It is argued that the social enterprise's financial sustainability and social mission are achieved through innovative business models. The integration of social finance and inclusion of patients with BOP as innovation elements in the business model innovation framework through the process of the business model change has been described. It is stated that the social finance invested in the equity capital ensures financial sustainability and guarantees the continuity in the healthcare services to patients with BOP, conforming to the perpetuity attribute of the cash waqf. The conceptual framework has also been positioned within the associated theoretical framework of sustainable social enterprise and business model and the work of others focusing on financial sustainability, social enterprise business model, and cash waqf. The conceptual framework explains how social finance invested in the equity capital funding of the social enterprise business model generates perpetuity, the most significant predictor of cash waqf.

7

THE IMPLEMENTATION OF THE SUSTAINABLE BUSINESS MODEL IN THE SOCIAL ENTERPRISE

In this chapter, we will focus on presenting the practical-applied aspects to the implementation of a healthcare business model of social enterprise. We will elaborate the action research cycles by explaining how the business model is innovated, what actions are taken to integrate the innovation through the business model change process, what outcome is achieved in the form of a new innovative business model, what challenges are encountered during the execution of the project. As already implicated, the action research method of this study begins with context, purpose, understanding and includes the four-step cycles— diagnosing, planning action, taking action, and evaluating action. This research method's essence is action, which develops experience. The objectives of the project are to develop and test a new healthcare business model of a social enterprise with shariah-based endowment investment through a business model innovation process and conduct a comparative study on medical treatment costs before and after the business model change.

The four cycles of action research are executed to integrate the innovation in the business model to develop a new innovative business model through business model change. The first cycle of the action research reviews the existing business model of the social enterprise through the lens of the business model canvas tool. The second cycle conducts the medical treatment of underprivileged patients and identifies the financial sustainability issue of the social enterprise. In this cycle, the conceptual framework of the business model innovation is conceived. The third cycle develops a social enterprise established on the conceptual framework of the business model innovation through the business model change. The fourth cycle validates the newly developed business model by conducting a comparative study on medical treatment costs before and after the business model change to verify the financial sustainability of the social enterprise. The outcome of the changes is described and discussed at the end of each cycle. Therefore, in each cycle, there are four subsections that clarify four phases of action research and discuss the results.

Figure 1. Presenting four cycles of action research cycles in the timeline

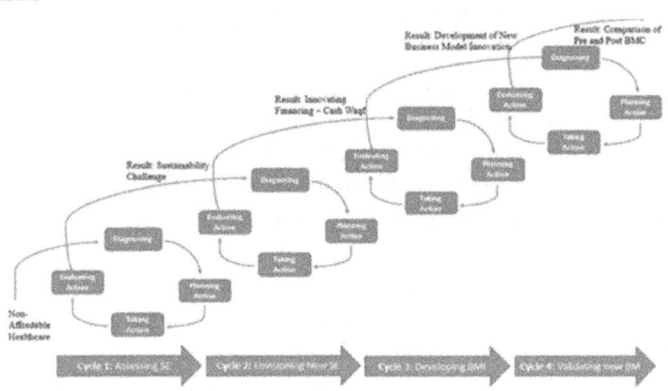

Assessment of the Existing Business Model of the Social Enterprise

While assessing the initial business model of the social enterprise business model, it is important to keep in mind that there are four cycles of action research, as stated earlier. In the first cycle of the action research, the association between the attributes of the existing business model of the social enterprise and the observed results is explored. In this cycle, the variations within attributes and differences in the severity of those attributes are closely correlated with trends in interest outcomes. The output here is referred to the challenges in the financial sustainability faced by the social enterprise. In this cycle of action research, the steps of identifying funding issues, planning fundraising, medical treatment, and review of the business model are conducted, and the financial output of social enterprise is achieved. The four steps of the first cycle are in the following Table 1 as seen in the next page:

Table 1. Assessment (immersion) healthcare business model

Phase of Action Research	Activity
Diagnosing	The funding issue to social enterprise is identified by reviewing the current business model, legal structure of the case firm, and understanding the business process of medical treatment of underprivileged patients at the social enterprise.
Action planning	An action plan to raise donations through an NGO to fund the medical treatment of underprivileged patients.
Action taking	The medical treatment of underprivileged patients with funding support from NGO, 300 patients, recommended for clinical study/trial in two phases (20 to 80 patients in the first phase and 100 to 200 patients in the second phase totaling to maximum 300 patients.
Evaluating Action	A study is conducted to review the business model of social enterprise with current financing support from the NGO.

The study on the existing legal structure of the case social enterprise reveals the fact that it is registered under Section 8 Company under Indian Companies Act 2013. A Section 8 Company is a company (for charitable or not-for-profit purposes) established 'for promoting commerce, art, science, sports, education, research, social welfare, religion, charity, protection of environment or any such other object', provided the profits, if any, or other income is applied for promoting only the objects of the company, and no dividend is paid to its members. The business process of the case social enterprise presented a straightforward healthcare service to the underprivileged segment. This business process provides a social enterprise typology that suggests possible business models. According to the logical structure of social relations between social enterprises, patients, and healthcare services offered, the specific business model that resulted from the nine fundamental types of business models for social enterprises is the type market intermediary model. The key advantage of the model is its potential for scalability by reaching out to underprivileged segments in different areas and ensuring a constant focus on the social mission; yet, it has self-financing limitations. The donation is the only revenue source and collected through a partner NGO. The entire proceeds of the donations were then utilized to deliver the medical service to the patients. The last phase of the evaluation of the first action research cycle generated the output from executing the business process in the form of the financial profit and loss account statement of the social enterprise. The output of the first action research cycle is fed as an entry point to the second action research cycle.

Verification of Sustainability Issue and Design of Business Model Innovation

In the second cycle of action research, the steps of verifying financial challenges, designing of business model innovation, raising social investment, and review of the conceptual framework are conducted with the input from the first action research cycle. The objective of the second action research cycle is to identify the financial sustainability challenges with the social enterprise and design a conceptual framework of business model innovation with social investment to address the financial sustainability issue. The social investors willing to fund the social enterprise with their social investments in equity capital funding are identified in this action research cycle. The four steps of the second action research cycle are in the following Table 2:

Table 2. Issue verification and envision of Business Model Innovation

Phase of Action Research	Activity
Diagnosing	Focus group discussion with the stakeholders of the social enterprise and reviewing the medical bills and financial profit and loss statement of the healthcare project;
Action planning	An action plan to design the conceptual framework of Business Model Innovation and identify social investors to provide capital funding to social enterprise;
Action taking	Raising social investments from high-net-worth individuals and retail investors to provide the capital funding;
Evaluating Action	A critical review of the conceptual framework for conformity of social investments raised as "cash waqf".

The SSEBM conceptual framework was analyzed for the conformity of the perpetuity attribute of the cash waqf. The new business model of the social enterprise with integration of financing innovation in the business model innovation through business model change ensured perpetuity of the cash waqf investment. Therefore, a fundraising campaign was designed to raise social finance in the form of cash waqf. The main objective of this fundraising was to raise public capital funds to support the social enterprise's financial sustainability and society's welfare. The case social enterprise working for the healthcare services and social welfare of the organization, also the sponsor of this action research study, submitted a business proposal to social investors of the Islamic investment community to join the new investment opportunity in the social enterprise.

The Islamic investment community is no stranger to the idea of venture philanthropy. Venture philanthropy is based on conventional venture-capital principles, but it is used in the Islamic sense to generate a financial and social return for Muslim societies. Returns from traditional venture capital funds are returned to investors. In contrast, returns from venture philanthropy funds are reinvested in the fund to allow it to grow its investment portfolio and its developmental effects. While conventional and venture philanthropy funds pursue capital from high-net-worth individuals and organizations, Shariah-compliant venture philanthropy funds concentrate on raising money from Sadaqah and cash waqf, the charitable donations from faithful Muslims. Shariah-based venture philanthropy provides a unique commodity that helps to harness the sophistication of contemporary social finance. Using the cash waqf method, successful businesspeople with capital and experience could become venture philanthropists. Therefore, individual Shariah-compliant venture philanthropists were introduced to the importance of direct cash waqf investment in capital funding to social enterprise. As a result of the investment proposal, the total investment commitment received were from 13 social investors (3 HNI & 10 Retail). There are notably two types of social investors- HNI social investors & retail social investors. Hence, the last phase of evaluation of the second action research cycle generated the social financing as output in the form of the cash waqf investment from the social investors. This output of the second action research cycle is fed as the starting point for the third action research cycle.

Development of the Healthcare Business Model with Social Investment

For the development of new healthcare social enterprise business model with social investment, we must address the second research objective - *"To develop a sustainable business model of healthcare social enterprise based on the Islamic concept of cash waqf investment to provide affordable health services in India",* in which a business model innovation is presented that suggested how to integrate innovative financing into the cycle of innovation in the business model. In the third cycle of this action research, the aim is to develop a new healthcare business model of a social enterprise with social investment through the theoretical concepts of business model innovation. The four steps of the third action research cycle are in Table 3, in the next page:

Table 3. Development of new healthcare social enterprise business model

Phase of Action Research	Activity
Diagnosing	Review of the legal structure of the SPE, review of equity capital funding structure, and review of the new healthcare business model after the business model change.
Action planning	An action plan to develop a new healthcare social enterprise business model through business model change process made by designing a new dual pricing structure (revenue model change in the theory of business model innovation), establishing new social enterprise with social equity financing (enterprise model change), and including patients with BOP in the consumer segment (industry model change).
Action taking	A new special purpose entity (SPE) is established with new social investors, structuring of the equity in SPE, and the documents to the legal council are submitted. The medical treatment of five hundred self-paying patients and five hundred patients with BOP.
Evaluating Action	A study is conducted to review the new healthcare social enterprise business model with current social financing support from social investors.

A special-purpose entity (SPE) unit is created within the case social enterprise. The change in the equity structure of the SPE unit brought a physical change in the social enterprise. The inclusion of social finance in equity capital funding, BOP patients, dual pricing, and teleconsulting innovation elements in the business model components during this change process presented the Business Model Innovation. The new healthcare social enterprise business after the business model change is represented with the business model canvas, as shown in Figure 2. The detail of business model component changed during is explained as follows:

- *Customer Segments:* In addition to the migrant worker, two new customer segments were added in the changed business model. The BOP segment, despite being with low spending and low budgets, is characterized by volumes. The second customer segment added was corporate or self-paying patients.

- *Value Proposition:* The additional value proposition was to offer Vitamin D home delivery. In the past, Vitamin D was only delivered through the medical center or mobile van. With the help of a distributor partner network, however, a new business model offered home delivery services of Vitamin D to accommodate more self-paying patients. The other value proposition was Teleconsulting that brought healthcare to those who, regardless of location, found it difficult to travel to a doctor or hospital, such as the disabled, the elderly, or those housed in institutions. Teleconsulting also gave a new source of revenue by extending the patient base and service offerings.

- *Key Resources:* Social finance in equity capital funding to the social enterprise was the key financial resource to the new business model. Equity partnerships were developed to ensure that these resources are accessible to the social enterprise. The financial resource component ensures the delivery of the value proposition to the customer segments and covers the impact cost of the social enterprise.

Figure 2. Business Model Canvas of NEW healthcare Social Enterprise

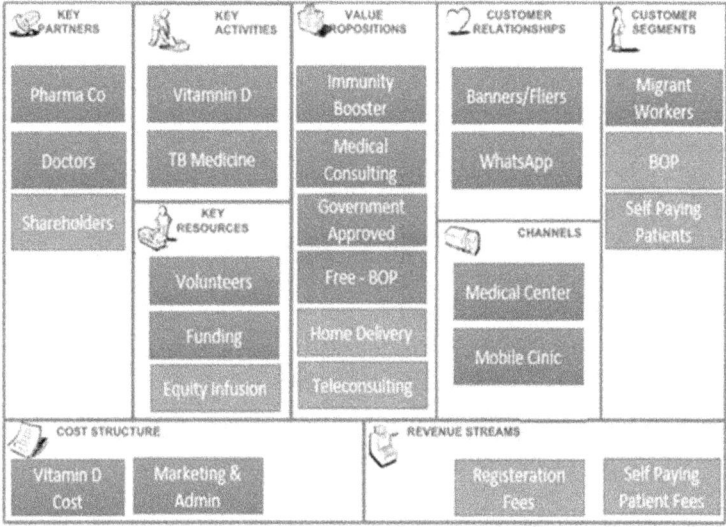

- *Key Partners:* Filling the continuous funding gap required the engagement of new shareholder partners to leverage additional financing. The ownership of shareholding in the social enterprise was done in full adherence to the Sharia principles. The social investors were the new key partners in the business model canvas.
- *Revenue Stream:* The new business model had two revenue streams, and each stream had different pricing mechanisms, such as registration fees and value-based fees for self-paying patients

In this third cycle of the action research, the innovation elements in enterprise, industry, and revenue model of business model innovation resulted in responses that changed the components of the business model. Through the integration of social finance in equity capital funding, BOP patients, dual pricing, and teleconsulting, the business model change process had inscribed the innovation elements into the business model innovation. These unique integrations of innovation elements in five components of the business model described the new business model. They described a sustainable financial and social sustainability of the healthcare social enterprise, distinct from the non-financially sustainable operation before the business model change had happened. This chain of transformation in the component of the business model is a process of the business model change. In this process, the prescription of innovation elements are drivers for change; the inscription into business model innovation is the material act of change, and the new healthcare business model described by the business model change is the result. The result from executing the business model change in the form of a new healthcare social enterprise business model was produced in the last evaluation phase of the third action research cycle.

Validation of a new Social Enterprise for Affordable Healthcare Services

In order to validate the financial sustainability of the new healthcare social enterprise business model, an empirical study was conducted in the fourth cycle of the action research. The validation of the social enterprise business model is essential for the application of social enterprise in practice. There are two characteristics that encourage the validation of the social enterprise business model in action research: Firstly, it enables testing in the application area directly. Secondly, it relies on the systematic diagnose-plan-act-evaluate of typical action research with practitioners, which ultimately allows the intended outcome attribute to be shaped and either accepted or rejected for further application. In the fourth cycle of the action research, the steps of identifying BOP patients, conducting a comparative study, medical treatment, and validating the affordable healthcare service were conducted at two different levels. The diagnosis at the first level of identifying the patients with BOP began in order to understand the common characteristics of the patients and identify issues related to affordability in healthcare treatment for the patients. The diagnostic output is the identification and selection of patients with BOP and self-paying patients that were used in the following three phases of the fourth action research cycle. The dual pricing mechanism was designed for two different segments of the patients. The registration fees were applicable to patients with BOP as well as self-paying patients.

Figure 3. Validation in Action Research Process

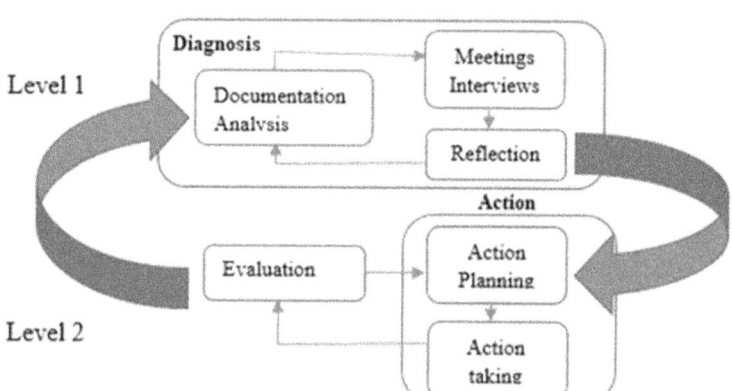

The action part of the research was organized at the second level, as shown in Figure 4, to utilize the new healthcare social enterprise business model for the treatment of the selected patients with BOP. Later, the input and comments of the participants were gathered to further confirm the affordability of the healthcare services to the patients with BOP. The four steps of the fourth cycle of action research to validate the new healthcare social enterprise business model are in the following Table 4:

Table 4. Validation of the New Social Enterprise Business Model

Phase of Action Research	Activity
Diagnosing	Focus group discussion with the stakeholders and interviewing social investors of the social enterprise and understanding the business process of medical treatment of patients with BOP at the social enterprise for the healthcare project executed after the business model change.
Action planning	An action plan to conduct a comparative study on medical treatment of Vitamin D and financial statements before and after the business model change.
Action taking	The medical treatment of 500 self-paying patients and 500 patients with BOP.
Evaluating Action	A comparative study of the medical treatment of self-paying patients and patients with BOP and financial statements are conducted to validate the affordable healthcare service to patients with BOP.

As shown in the figure below, the invoice from the pharmaceutical company supplying the Vitamin D and medical bills from the patients were collected. The balance sheet and profit and loss account statement of the Vitamin D project executed by the new healthcare social enterprise was reviewed. The revenue generated from the self-paying patients of the new healthcare social enterprise and surplus was utilized to deliver the Vitamin D vial and health services to the patients with BOP. Focus group discussions with social enterprise stakeholders and interviews of social investors were conducted to validate and confirm the accessibility and affordability of Vitamin D and delivering healthcare services to patients with BOP.

Figure 4. New Social Enterprise Healthcare Services Delivery

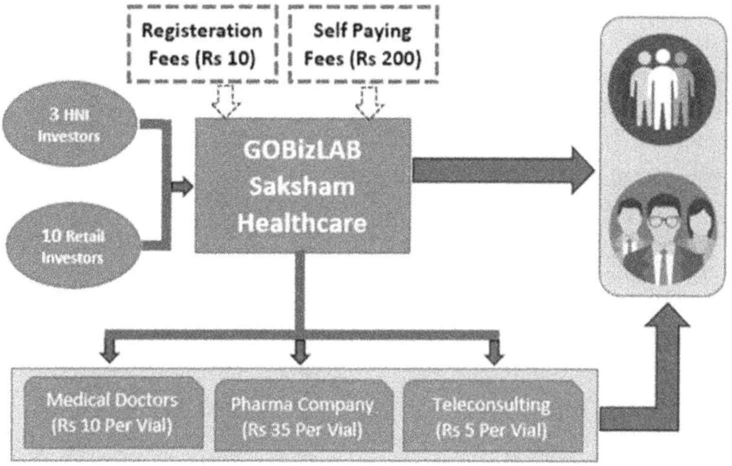

![Figure 4 diagram: GOBizLAB Saksham Healthcare receives Registration Fees (Rs 10) and Self Paying Fees (Rs 200), backed by 3 HNI Investors and 10 Retail Investors, delivering services via Medical Doctors (Rs 10 Per Vial), Pharma Company (Rs 35 Per Vial), and Teleconsulting (Rs 5 Per Vial) to patients.]

The comparative effectiveness study to compare the efficacy of two or more medical treatments for healthcare social enterprise was used in the evaluation phase. In this evaluation phase of the fourth action research cycle, the comparative effectiveness framework was used to conduct the cost comparison of the billing of self-paying and patients with BOP. Comparative effectiveness analysis of the medical bills of the healthcare delivery system identifies efficiency at the service level, primarily cost efficiency, for self-paying patients with BOP.

The evolution of the first action research cycle presented the business model of the healthcare social enterprise, and the second action research cycle revealed the financial sustainability issue of the healthcare social enterprise, which allowed the researcher to reflect and realize that further action research cycles are required. The conceptual framework of business model innovation is developed in the third cycle and then validated in the fourth cycle by conducting action research. The chapter also delivers knowledge imparted from the fourth cycle of action research; the innovative financing can broaden the perspective of affordable healthcare, hence increasing possibilities to provide healthcare services to patients with BOP by changing business model elements.

This chapter has validated the conceptual framework for integrating financial sustainability in the healthcare social enterprise business model. The action research is participatory and collaborative in nature, and it benefits both the social enterprise and the research. The study was an empirical application of the conceptual framework in an Indian social enterprise focused on healthcare services. The case social enterprise was offering healthcare services in partnership with NGO and was raising donations along with offering healthcare services to the patients with BOP. In order to provide continuous affordable healthcare services, the conceptual framework was implemented to make the case social enterprise financially sustainable using the business model innovation approach through the business model change process. The action research approach for case social enterprise was conducted in four phases, including two business model mapping using a business model canvas tool in the first assessment and third development phase. The innovative social finance was brought into the capital element of the social enterprise business model, and healthcare services offered to patients with BOP resulted in a business model innovation framework. The new business model demonstrated profitability that was being used to offer free healthcare services to patients with BOP bringing perpetuity to the social finance investment.

8

SUSTAINABLE SOCIAL ENTERPRISE WITH CASH WAQF INVESTMENT

An analysis of learning experiences as a result of overall reflection and data collected through interviews, focus group meetings, and reflective journals in relation to the research questions have been presented in this chapter. It discusses the findings that emerged from the four action research cycles and the relation with relevant theoretical aspects, especially from the social enterprises, financial sustainability of social enterprises, and shariah-based endowment investment. The objective was to analyze the aspects that became apparent in a detailed manner to describe the social enterprise transformation from non-profit aspects to more financially sustainable and affordable healthcare that form the basis for a business model innovation to function. The focused group discussions with the social investors of the social enterprise were carried out from June 2021 to October 2021. The focused group discussion was conducted through in-person meetings to collect data from social investors of the case social enterprise. They were interviewed using certain questions specifically related to the motivations of the social investors to invest the cash waqf in the social enterprise, the cost-effectiveness of the medical treatment, and experience of working with the healthcare social enterprise in India.

Characteristics of the Participants

The selection of interviewees was a crucial decision-making process for researchers conducting a qualitative study. Some of the primary considerations for selecting interviewees in this study were determining the number of interviews necessary and the method for selecting each individual interviewee. Considering that the intention of inductive research was theory-building rather than theory-testing, the selection of interviewees was not determined by concern for delegation of an overall population. Instead, it was shaped by purposive theoretical sampling that targets a conceptual inquiry and helps to achieve information richness. The interviewees were social investors. Socio-demographic characteristics such as age, level of education, awareness of shariah-compliant investment, and amount of funds under management were used.

The critical parameter for HNI social investors was involvement and experience in Sharia-based waqf investment in their career history. The members of Islamic institutions and decision-making arrangements, strategy and advisory groups, steering committees, investments and funding boards, and arrangements related to Shariah-compliant businesses were considered. Due to the nature of this study, the author focused on individuals who had considerable experience in Islamic finance. Participants needed to have experience with Islamic finance so that they could comment on it in retrospect. The interviewees needed to have experience of at least one successful and/or poor investment, which meant that the decisions either succeeded or they failed but were examined in retrospect. Following the research objectives, out of HNI social investors participants, three individuals involved in Islamic finance investments for enterprises with multi-million rupees in investment portfolio per year were considered. Moreover, in order to have a holistic view, the interviewees had experience with successful and unsuccessful decisions made under social finance to commercial and social enterprises. Further, ten retail social investors who were highly qualified and had experience in investing in social enterprises were interviewed.

Analysis of the Qualitative Data

Semi-structured interviews, field notes, and documentation presented by participants were the data collection techniques used in this study that provided a degree of triangulation. All interviews with the participants were recorded in a secured document. The interviews offered the author the opportunity to analyze in greater detail the data found in the financial statements of the social enterprise before and after the business model change. In general, there are two kinds of data analysis— theoretical & empirical. By gathering both empirical and qualitative data, the researcher was more likely to gain a good understanding of the phenomena being examined and to be able to explain and validate the conclusions drawn from it. The interview questions were developed with the intention of uncovering the views and expectations of social investors on the process and outcomes of the new healthcare social enterprise business model in the areas of practicality, validity, sustainability, continued practice, and healthcare services. The validity of the results of the interviews were also supported by conducting the analysis of the financial data collected from the new healthcare social enterprise, which brought similar findings. The results of the interviews, financial data analysis, and reflection provided insights into affordable healthcare through the newly developed healthcare social enterprise business model. These results support the claim that the social enterprise business model with cash waqf investment is a viable concept based on business model innovation that social enterprises and society can accept and not just a pure, unsubstantiated theory made up by academics.

The phenomenological method was used to analyze the interview data on qualitative analysis and interpretation. The main aim of the analysis was to arrange responses in such a way that trends were established, and general patterns were clear. The interview data was organized by themes that arose from the interview questions and responses. In each set of responses for every theme, notable remarks were found for later quotations and quantifying details where possible. Through holding up the phenomenon of action research for analysis, taken from the context in which it exists and carefully dissected, it was possible to discover, describe, and examine its components and basic structures of the new social enterprise business model in the healthcare setting. The objective of the interview analysis was to identify the motivations of social investors to invest in the development of the new healthcare social enterprise business model for affordable healthcare.

Social Mission Influencing Cash Waqf Investment in the Social Enterprise

In the social enterprise, a social mission influences the cash waqf investment. The first major theme that emerged from the data was the social mission of the social enterprise. Well, the social mission is the factor that influences the decisions and behavior of social investors involved in the development of the new healthcare business model of the social enterprise. It consists of two constructs which influence the motivation of social investors. These constructs ultimately influence the investment decision, which sets the social investor's investment goal. They include solving societal healthcare problems and the affordability of healthcare services. Social investors are individuals who are involved in the development of social enterprise decision-making arrangements, and the investment goal is the key for these individuals, which in turn is determined by their social mission. In other words, this social mission shapes the investment goal. This data gathered from this study demonstrates the factors that influence the social mission of individual social investors involved in decision-making before the decisions are made. The first construct to emerge from the social mission is healthcare societal need. The significance of a societal need describes the scope of a problem that a social enterprise seeks to solve. The data suggests that this construct speaks to an understanding of society's needs that participants believe must be in place for successful social enterprise. The participants approached the social mission— which shapes the social investment goal and is influenced by healthcare societal need— as a possibility, and an opportunity that allows for soundness and trustworthy future social enterprises.

Anonymous Participant 1, who is the Promoter Director of an investment advisory and portfolio management firm, identified the social mission of their investment as "Very much healthcare-centric." In this way, all social enterprises and their business models are viewed through that lens: "The healthcare industry is undergoing a global transformation. Demographic trends in India, such as aging populations and rising poverty levels, are reshaping individuals' and governments' health priorities. This is bringing a new wave of social investment, with the purpose of social investors investing in solving healthcare problems."

Similarly, Anonymous Participant 2, who is the Head of Investment of a large Auto Finance company, depicted how healthcare needs to play a crucial role when identifying the reasons for making social investment decisions. In this case, the healthcare needs of the society were described as follows: "The healthcare system of the Indian government is ineffective in meeting social healthcare needs. The healthcare of common people should be a necessity." The investment goal is influenced by the healthcare societal needs and the social mission to get there. The participant described: "For nearly 15 years, the government of India's health spending has been stuck at roughly 1% of GDP, and shortly, the situation seems unlikely to improve. Adequate investments are needed to ensure any health emergency for the common people. Therefore, the social investor should tap into the potential of social enterprise with a mission to address the society's critical need."

The participants emphasized the importance of a social mission in the development of social enterprise driven by healthcare societal needs, arguing that either a lack of such a social mission or the communication of a cohesive and consistent social mission can affect the success of the development of social enterprise. Frequently, participants noted the challenges of needing a crystal-clear social mission. Such a clear social mission leads to consistency in action and, ideally, results. Societal healthcare needs to shape this social mission. This book proposes that:

Proposition 1: Healthcare societal needs shape the investment goal by providing social investors a better understanding of the social mission.

Affordable healthcare services were another construct extracted from the social mission theme. Delivering affordable healthcare services to communities, especially BOP, is a prerequisite for poverty reduction. Social enterprises have emphasized their social mission, such as poverty alleviation, through affordable healthcare services built into their business strategy. Regarding social investors, affordability surfaces as the central construct that must serve BOP patients' use of social enterprise. The data highlights the need for social enterprises to deliver affordable healthcare services and, in general, to attract better social investors to participate in developing the healthcare social enterprise business model with their social investment. The relative importance of this construct was highlighted by several respondents, who described affordability as a primary dimension when it came to a successful social enterprise. High healthcare prices and the risk of catastrophic healthcare expenditures play a significant role in BOP patients' choice of healthcare provider, affecting social investors' investment criteria. Anonymous Participant 3, who is the Vice President of an Information technology company specializing in FinTech sectors, said: "In India, the lack of affordable and quality healthcare services is a major issue for the underprivileged community. We finance healthcare access because we see enormous potential to support innovative, low-cost models that make healthcare more accessible and inexpensive for BOP while benefiting from the Indian healthcare system's increasing gaps between demand and supply."

Anonymous Participant 4, who is the Promoter Director of an investment advisory and portfolio management firm, concurred, noting that social investors should invest according to the fit with the social mission set by the BOP's actual healthcare needs. The challenges of having the unaffordable cost of healthcare services to BOP patients can change the interest of social investors. This study found that social investments could be attracted to social missions resulting from affordable healthcare services to BOP patients. So, this book proposes that:

Proposition 2: Affordable healthcare services to BOP patients influence the investment goal by providing social investors with a clear social mission while making an investment decision.

This book sought to identify from the perspective of social investors involved in developing the healthcare business model of the social enterprise. The social investor's view of investment decision-making indicates that social investors not only make decisions regarding social investment but also decide what healthcare needs to prioritize when making decisions related to social investments. The social mission influencing social investors' decisions originates from the investment goal. This study found that social investors' decisions are influenced by their investment goals shaped by their perspectives of social enterprise's capability in addressing the healthcare societal needs, as illustrated in proposition.

1. In addition, the social enterprise's ability to offer affordable healthcare services to BOP patients is also considered by the social investor. It influences how

social investors approach and make decisions regarding social investments, as presented in proposition 2

2. The inclusion of BOP patients enables an understanding of the social mission. The social enterprise needed to consider including BOP patients, ensuring continuous and affordable healthcare services to influence social investors' investment goals. Overall, the study revealed that the investment decision-making of social investors primarily depended on the social mission of the social enterprise. As such, although factors required for decision-making were available to the social investors, the interconnection among factors' attributes that may formulate decisions remained tacit and thus required codification. As a result, the rationale for decisions needed to be explained, followed consistently, and was risk-adequate.

Sustainable Business Model as a Driver for Affordable Healthcare

It is vital to note that the sustainable business model aims to provide affordable healthcare. After the social mission, the sustainable business model is the second theme identified in the data, where social investors shape investment decisions. Constructs in this theme include financial sustainability and innovation. Participants in this study were both aware of and able to describe what they had perceived in developing the healthcare social enterprise stage with their investment. While participants occasionally described the development process by which the social investments were integrated to achieve a sustainable business model of the social enterprise, their focus was the affordability of the healthcare services. The data shows that before the investment decision is made, social investors' choices between multiple decision options are influenced by the sustainable business model of the social enterprise, which is shaped through financial sustainability and innovation in the business model. Financial sustainability is the first construct to emerge from the sustainable business model theme. It describes how likely social enterprise will achieve financial goals.

They use a sustainable business model to cut down on healthcare expenses and generate adequate economic resources to assure long-term financial sustainability. In terms of financial sustainability, the participants agreed that social enterprises should be able to attract social investors when financial sustainability means that the social enterprise generates enough cash to cover its operating costs and possibly even a profit. The financial sustainability of the newly developed healthcare social enterprise was initially supported through the social investment in equity capital funding, and after the development of the sustainable business model, the financial sustainability was realized through the dual price mechanism. Anonymous Participant 5, who is the Chief Financial Officer of a large investment bank, described the role of financial sustainability through a sustainable business model, adding:

"Outcome monitoring is considerably more difficult and critical for social enterprises with a double bottom line to answer for. Proving social impact and demonstrating financial sustainability is key to building a sustainable business model and attracting social investments. Generating profit from the self-paying patients and leveraging the surplus to offer the affordable healthcare services to BOP patients with dual pricing strategy is an innovative idea of the social healthcare enterprise."

For Anonymous Participant 6, who is the Cost Accountant of a Chartered Accountant firm, the financial sustainability was not just to attract the social investor to invest capital funding to social enterprise, but also a determination of improving the socio-economic conditions of the BOP communities through affordable healthcare services.

The data says that financial sustainability needs to be achieved for a social enterprise's business model to be considered sustainable. This could be achieved with a dual-price mechanism for regular patients and BOP patients. So, this book proposes that:

Proposition 3: Social enterprises are more likely to provide affordable healthcare services if the business model development involves financial sustainability.

Innovation was another construct extracted from the sustainable business model theme. The ability to innovate is critical to a social enterprise's definition. It refers to how the social enterprise approaches a societal problem in a novel way. Participants pointed specifically to how innovation influences the sustainable business model that sets their investment goal, which in turn allows a social investor to make a decision and take risks in their social investment without worrying about the profit of the social enterprise. Anonymous Participant 7, who is the Innovation Director of a large Information Technology Company, used the example of Narayana Healthcare to demonstrate the role of innovation in the sustainable business model: "Narayana Health is a proven business model with frugal innovation delivering high-quality healthcare services at a cheaper cost, thereby attracting access to social investments. Innovations are the key drivers of today's sustainable business model, and this is one of the factors that makes healthcare social enterprises attractive investments for social investors."

This book found that innovation can be integrated into the business model at different levels. Innovation with which a business model needs to be integrated could be at an operation, strategic, and economic status. For example, in the case of operational-level innovation, there are variations in the services offered and multiple modes of service delivery for each user segment to ensure affordable healthcare services. Anonymous Participant 8, who is the Director of a Mumbai based Medical Device company said: "To sustainably satisfy patients' needs, innovative solutions that change people's lives through products, services, processes, and business models are required. The healthcare social enterprises that combine telemedicine innovation with low-cost medications to provide affordable care to patients who are underserved by traditional healthcare providers are preferred by the social investors."

Technological innovative advancements improve the delivery of healthcare services. As a result, investments in social enterprise are aimed at enhancing the creative and innovative capabilities of the social enterprise. The literature emphasized the importance of the nexus between technology and social enterprise in improving the innovativeness of a social enterprise and the importance of these two factors in influencing investors' decisions. Regardless of the level of the innovation, it is a construct that controls the sustainable business model because it provides the social enterprise with an opportunity to ensure the delivery of affordable healthcare, aiding social enterprises in achieving social investment goals. This study found that innovation helps social enterprises take steps towards delivering affordable healthcare services even when the profit needs to be completely clear. So, it is proposed that:

Proposition 4: Affordable healthcare services will improve if social enterprises integrate innovation into their sustainable business model.

The next stage of the analysis is to theorize a conceptual framework. Two empirical themes and four constructs were abstracted from the data. Figure 1 presents a graphic illustration of the sustainable social enterprise business model employed in this study. It depicts the relationship between social investment and sustainability of the social enterprise business model and the various factors involved in attaining financial sustainability while providing affordable healthcare services to BOP patients from social investments in equity capital funding to social enterprise. This model also explains how the integration of innovation leads to affordable healthcare services for BOP patients. The evolving sustainable social enterprise business model theory is based on the original theory of financial sustainability, social enterprise business model, and cash waqf. Due to the intuitive nature of the evolving theory of sustainable social enterprise business model, a graphical representation of the overall theoretical process is used as a rhetorical device to trigger epiphanies.

Figure 1. Theoretical Model: Sustainable Social Enterprise Business Model

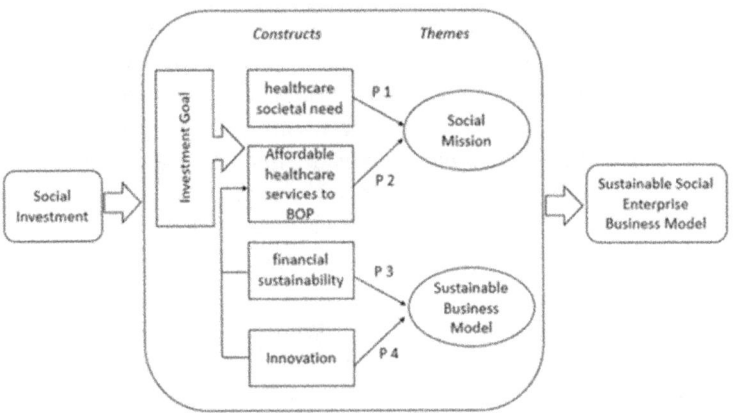

The model shows that from the perspective of social investors involved in the development of the healthcare business model of the social enterprise, social investment decision-making consists of a preliminary element of the social mission followed by the sustainable business model of the social enterprise. The decision-making process undertaken by social investors involved various constructs that underpin a sustainable business model, from the consideration of financial sustainability to innovation to offer affordable healthcare services. Propositions 3 and 4 describe the relationship between the two key constructs. Identification of social investors' motivation depends on the factors influencing the financial sustainability of the social enterprise. In this case, when making decisions related to a social enterprise that offers affordable healthcare services, the social investors consider a business model that involves financial sustainability, as presented in proposition 3. With social enterprises having a social mission that included BOP patients, the success of their sustainable business model is dependent on how social enterprises delivered affordable healthcare services. This model advanced the importance of a sustainable business model for the decision-making related to social investments by social investors. The development of a sustainable social enterprise business model was a process that aimed to deliver affordable healthcare services, which was achieved through integrating innovation into the business model of social enterprise. In conclusion, the phenomenological study identified four new constructs and four propositions in an inductive theory-building process. The four propositions developed through the interviews of the social investors are found reasonably valid and reliable and derived from the characterization of the social investment in the equity capital funding of the social enterprise. The phenomenological study built a new theory explaining the sustainability of the social enterprise business model from the perspective of the social investor and uniquely showed how a sustainable social enterprise business model attained financial sustainability and delivered affordable and continuous healthcare services to BOP patients.

Analysis of the Empirical Investigation

As already mentioned earlier, the analysis of data is done in two ways—- Theoretical (with qualitative data) & Empirical. We have learnt about the analysis of theoretical data. Now, we shall move on to the Empirical investigation. In this research, empirical evidence has been used in the form of a financial report as a data source to assist in addressing the research question. When handled carefully, financial documents can be a rich source of knowledge and information for social research. The researcher reviewed the publicly available financial reports to corroborate this information with the information provided by the participants during the interview. In this section, the approach used to answer the research question through the comparative financial data analysis collected from the healthcare social enterprise before and after the business model change has been described. The financial data, which included profit & loss account statements, were collected from the case healthcare social enterprise. The data in Table 1. illustrates the summary of profit and loss account of the case healthcare social enterprise before the business model change in June 2021 and after in October 2021.

Table 1. Income & Expense Sheet

Particulars	Before Business Model Change June 2021		After Business Model Change October 2021	
	Units	Amount	Units	Amount
Income				
Donation	15	16,300		
BOP Registration Fees			500	5,000
Self-Paying Patient Fees			500	100,000
Total Income		16,300		105,000
Expenses				
Cost of Vitamin D Vial	300	10,500	500	35,000
Medical Doctor Fees		3,000		10,000
Teleconsulting App Charges			500	5,000
Administrator Fees		1,000		5,000
Campaign Banner & Flier		1,000		4,000
Fundraising Expense		800		
Vial Distribution Charges			500	10,000
Total Expenses		16,300		69,000
Change in Net Assets		0		36,000

The income to healthcare social enterprise, prior to business model change in June 2021, was only through the donation raised by the partner NGO on the crowdfunding web portal (www.ketto.org). The entire fund received by the case healthcare social enterprise was completely utilized to deliver the healthcare services to the underprivileged patients, as shown in Figure 2 of Chapter 5 and confirmed in the third column of Table 1. In October 2021, the financial data was collected again after the business model change. The objective of the data collection was to analyze the effect of business model change on the financial operation of the healthcare social enterprise. The financial data showed that there was a significant increase in both revenue and profit margin of the case healthcare social enterprise discussed and justified in the sections that follow. More specifically, with the business model innovation of the case healthcare social enterprise through the business model change process, the profit margin as a percentage was higher than prior to the change in the business model.

Inclusive Healthcare Services Delivery to the Bottom of the Pyramid

Usually, there are inclusive healthcare services available for BOP patients. The key building block of the overall business model innovation of any social enterprise includes economic, operational, and strategic approaches. The financial data and documents collected from the case healthcare social enterprise are analyzed with respect to the approach being taken across these building blocks. The case healthcare social enterprise focused on providing Vitamin D Vial to the BOP that was affordable, accessible, had the proper product and was accompanied by a government scheme of promoting preventive tuberculosis (TB) medicine. Any BOP solution had to eliminate the accessibility, affordability, availability, and product/service-quality mix restrictions, and the case healthcare social enterprise operating at the BOP recognized it.

Regarding the economic approach, case healthcare social enterprise ensured a good mix of self-paying and BOP patients in order to achieve cross-subsidization. A cross-subsidization model encourages an organizational structure in which self-paying patients pay a greater price for a product or service than BOP patients, who pay lower prices for the same product or service. The 50% of case social enterprise's patients are self-paying and pay for their Vitamin D Vial and associated healthcare consultancy services, while the remaining 50% are paid minimal registration fees. Affluent or Self-paying patients get better support, such as 24X7 doctor consultancy instead of delivery-time consultancy for BOP patients, home-delivery of Vitamin D Vial, and teleconsulting mobile application. However, the healthcare social enterprise provides the same Vitamin D Vial to every single patient and constantly provides the same doctor's service between self-paying and BOP patients. The case healthcare social enterprise designed its pricing on a "dual pricing" model where BOP patients were charged only registration fees, providing an opportunity to BOP patients to access quality healthcare service. The cumulative cost of Vitamin D Vial, as shown in Table 2, for BOP patients is less than self-paying patients by about 95%. The financial report data revealed that the case healthcare social enterprise provided Vitamin D Vial to BOP patients at no cost, while the doctor's fees were waived off. The data analysis of the case healthcare social enterprise revealed their use of cross-subsidization, where the revenue from the self-paying patients who paid full charges of Rs. 200 was used to cross-subsidize the charges of BOP patients who could not pay the full charges.

Table 2. Cross-Subsidization of Medical Expenditure in INR.

Patients Type → Cost Items	Self-Paying Patients	BOP Patients
Registration Fees	10	10
Doctors Fee	10	
Vitamin D Vial	35	
Teleconsulting App	5	
Distribution Charges	10	
Others	130	
Total	**200**	**10**

Regarding the operational approach, case healthcare social enterprise adopted cost control as a prime objective in their operational strategy. The case social enterprise achieved the same by focusing on the cost optimization on the supply and delivery side both such as having procurement of Vitamin D vial directly from the pharmaceutical company than medical distributors, replacing professional freight delivery agents with hiring local delivery boys, using open-source inventory management software for inventory and distribution management. Other operational strategy measures included focusing on training local poor but educated girls as nurses for injecting the Vitamin D vial if required. Other cost-control measures included bulk procurement contracts with suppliers to have increased bargaining power. On the delivery side, use of mobile clinic vans equipped with nurses for implementing a Walk-in model to provide cost-effective access to Vitamin D treatment for BOP patient people living in slum areas. This Walk-in approach contributed significantly to bridging the accessibility gap for BOP patients while also distributing the load factor across multiple levels of the self-paying patients. The case healthcare social enterprise went a step further by organizing preventive healthcare camps, such as tuberculosis awareness and diagnosis, to supplement their value offers.

Regarding the strategic approach, the medical bills of certain patients were analyzed before and after the business model change. The empirical data was used for comparative cost-effectiveness analysis to determine the affordability of the healthcare services offered by the case healthcare social enterprise to the BOP patients before and after the business model change, as illustrated in Table 3.

Table 3. Patients with BOP and Self-Paying patients' Medical Treatment Costs

Before Business Model Change			After Business Model Change		
	Patient Type	Bill Amount		Patient Type	Bill Amount
Patient 1	U	0	Patient 1	B	10
Patient 2	U	0	Patient 2	B	10
Patient 3	U	0	Patient 3	S	200
Patient 4	B	0	Patient 4	S	200
Patient 5	U	0	Patient 5	B	10

Notes: U denotes underprivileged patients. B denotes patients with BOP. S denotes Self-paying patients.

Table 3. presented a breakdown of the costing structure for patients with BOP and self-paying patients treated before and after the business model change. Before the business model changed, the social enterprise offered Vitamin D vial for free to all the segments of the society. This free distribution included the underprivileged, patients with BOP, and patients who could pay the bill. After the business model change, the case healthcare social enterprise included BOP patients in their consumer segment and designed an innovative pricing scheme to offer the Vitamin D vial with only registration fees to the patients with BOP. The cost comparison revealed that the charges to BOP Patients were 95% less than the self-paying patients. This study used financial reports and medical billing of case healthcare social enterprise to unravel business model innovation strategies for inclusive healthcare at BOP. The empirical data highlighted that economic, operational, and strategic approaches are the core strategies that underpin the success of the social mission of the case healthcare social enterprise through business model innovation.

Equity Financing as a Strategy for Sustainability of the Social Enterprise

Equity financing is a great strategy for the sustainability of social enterprises. The objective of collecting the financial report of the case healthcare social enterprise was the measurement of social enterprise performance after the business model change from a financial sustainability perspective. The question after the business model change was how was the case of healthcare social enterprise performing from a financial perspective with the injection of equity financing in the form of cash waqf, so profitability, liquidity, and financing indicators were analyzed. For the period of June to October 2021, synthetic financial statements were compiled, and balance sheet indicators and profit and loss ratios were produced for the study.

In terms of financial profitability, in June 2021, the case of social enterprise was at breakeven. October 2021, after the business model change, brought an increase in profitability for the case social enterprise. The average turnover, as illustrated in Table 1 above, increased in October 2021 by 84 percent. The case social enterprises, which use an innovative business model to provide healthcare services for BOP communities, constituted a unique business strategy. The profit and loss statement indicated that the case social enterprise was good at generating income and accumulating reserves. It also demonstrated that the business model is sustainable after the business model changes, and the case of healthcare social enterprise is financially astute and sustainable.

In terms of liquidity, the case social enterprise incorporated as Section (8) companies presented an average liquidity ratio of 1 in June 2021, maintaining to 1 in October 2021. Liquidity ratios are a type of financial indicator that is used to assess an organization's capacity to repay current obligations. The majority of social enterprises have a liquidity ratio of around 1, indicating a cash flow situation that is frequently strained. In October 2021, the case healthcare social enterprise employed net assets in the aggregate amount of Rs. 16,36,000, as shown in the balance sheet in Table 4. A social enterprise's balance sheet is a declaration of the organization's net worth as of a specific date. The difference between what an enterprise has and what it owes is its net value. The case healthcare social enterprise presented positive capital for the analyzed period. Liquidity risk is one of the most important risks to affect the sustainability of social enterprises. Therefore, it is worthwhile to consider an evaluation of liquidity risk of the case social enterprise using Basel III and Solvency II accords that aim to ensure sufficient regulatory capital is held by enterprises to reinforce liquidity risk management. Basel III guidelines offer two measures to mitigate liquidity risk: Liquidity Coverage Ratio (LCR) and Net Stable Funding Ratio (NSFR). These two ratios have to be greater than 100 percent. The calculation of LCR and NSFR of the case social enterprise showed 64% and 26%, respectively, posing no liquidity risk.

Table 4. Balance Sheet of Social Enterprise after the Business Model Change

Assets		Liabilities and Equity	
Current Assets		**Current Liabilities**	
Cash	21,000	Total liabilities	0
Investments	16,00,000	**Net Equity**	
Prepaid Expenses	5,000	Share Capital	16,00,000
Account Receivables	10,000	Retained Earnings	36,000
Subtotal	16,36,000	Subtotal	16,36,000
Total Assets	**16,36,000**	**Total Liabilities and Equity**	**16,36,000**

The case healthcare social enterprise also benefited from the non-commercial revenues. The majority came from capital such as social financing. An important indicator that shows capital funding in terms of social finance is cash waqf investment. The case healthcare social enterprise had three high net worth individual (HNI) social investors as majority shareholders, while two shareholders were founders with a social mission. The case social enterprise provided opportunities for sustainable revenues for BOP communities and utilized the cash waqf investment for the working capital of the enterprise. It is important to note that within the case of social enterprise, the social mission prevailed over the economic purpose. The case social enterprise represented that it worked with the most vulnerable communities, BOP patients.

The case healthcare social enterprise used innovative funding strategies in the form of cash waqf investment that supported and leveraged balance sheets in order to be sustainable and deliver a social impact. Healthy balance sheets ensured social financing and, as a result, supported social enterprise's affordable healthcare to the BOP patients. To remain sustainable, the case healthcare social enterprise evolved through the business model change process integrating innovative social financing in its business model. The equity funding in the form of cash waqf investment brought better management of the balance sheet and therefore increased the social impact of the case social enterprise, which was the ultimate mission.

Thus, this chapter has outlined the overall data collected from the individual interviews with the social investors and focus groups with the stakeholders that have been conducted. The detailed results and analysis of the data have also been theorized and discussed. The analysis was also based on further investigation and the study that included the financial data collected from the new healthcare social enterprise. The data and outcomes of this analysis, the equity capital funding to healthcare social enterprise business model bringing the financial sustainability and offering continuous affordable healthcare services to patients with BOP conforming to the perpetuity attribute of the cash waqf, helped to validate and answer the research question. Also, these findings enabled the fulfillment of the research objectives aimed at this study, in this book.

CONCLUSION

Since we have reached the end of the book, we shall summarize the major conclusions drawn from the research and compare them with the objectives of the study and the questions it was aimed to answer. There is an analysis of the theoretical and empirical contributions that were made. Not only this, the research gaps that motivated the study, as well as how they were addressed during the research, are mentioned while discussing the contributions of the study. The conceptual and action research limitations shall also be discussed. Well, this is helpful in pinpointing the researcher's experiences that influenced the study's completion inside the research setting. Further to this, future research possibilities will also be identified. This shall assist other researchers in directing their attention to topics which were not included in the study, but that should be investigated in order to further understanding.

Addressing research question

The data collected in the previous chapter answered the research question: "What explains the investment in equity capital funding to a sustainable social enterprise healthcare business model to be a cash waqf"? The aforementioned research question was answered by formulating two objectives. The first research objective of the study was to substantiate the role of investment in equity capital funding to social enterprise as a factor for financial sustainability. The conceptual inquiry in chapter four sought to address this objective by proposing an innovative business model of a healthcare social enterprise that seeks investment in equity capital funding. At the same time, this conceptual inquiry addressed the manner in which innovative financing in the business model can facilitate the attainment of financial sustainability through business model change. To this end, the conceptual study provided a conceptual framework that introduced and described the sustainable business model of healthcare social enterprise. The conceptual model has then been developed and tested in an action research study, which was the second objective of the study.

The second research objective of the study was to develop a sustainable business model of healthcare social enterprise based on the Islamic concept of cash waqf investment to provide affordable and continuous health services in India. Various components of business model innovation, such as social finance in the form of cash waqf investment, dual pricing, and BOP segment, all lead to bringing innovation to the business model for financial sustainability. The action research inquiry sought to address the second objective by integrating innovation in the healthcare business model to develop a new innovative business model through business model change. The outcome from implementing business model innovation as a result of integrating innovative financing through a business model change process across four action research cycles was addressed as a sustainable social enterprise business model (SSEBM). In order to testify to the proposed conceptual framework of SSEBM, an empirical study was conducted in the fourth cycle of action research. Most importantly, the findings of the study are derived from an empirical study on business model innovation, which in the past used to be only based on the study of the conceptual model.

The empirical data analysis confirms that the healthcare services offered by the newly developed social enterprise after the business model change with social investment has improved the quality of the healthcare and provided low cost, affordable, and continuous healthcare for all, especially patients with BOP. A portion of the profit generated by social enterprise was utilized to fund the free healthcare service to patients with BOP. The continuity in the healthcare services to patients with BOP conformed to the perpetuity in benefiting the society, a critical attribute of the waqf. As such, the perpetuity attribute in waqf intends to serve as means to receive the continuous reward, even after death, for the social investors. This explains why social investment made in equity capital funding to a sustainable social enterprise healthcare business model can be considered cash waqf.

Thereafter, the study provided evidence of investing criteria of social investment from an individual perspective, which supported the decision-making of the cash waqf in the equity capital funding of the sustainable social enterprise business model. As a result, the study developed a theoretical model sustainable social enterprise business model (SSEBM) derived from four drivers— two drivers of the social mission are the ability of SSEBM to solve healthcare societal problems and deliver affordable and continuous healthcare services & two drivers of a sustainable business model are financial sustainability and innovation. The affordable and continuous healthcare services are depicted in the value proposition and value delivery component of the SSEBM, whereas cash waqf in equity capital funding and inclusion of BOP segment act as part of the innovation element of the sustainable business model of SSEBM.

Contribution to the theory

As mentioned previously, this study sets out to address research gaps in the business model and sustainable social enterprise literature related to the financial sustainability of social enterprise through the social investment in equity capital funding. As such, this research addressed the gaps that were outlined and identified by answering the question, "What explains the investment in equity capital funding to a sustainable social enterprise healthcare business model to be a cash waqf"? In order to address this question, the research described a clear conceptualization of the sustainable social enterprise business model. It proposed a conceptual framework that provided a better understanding of the manner in which innovative financing in the form of cash waqf is integrated into the business model. Furthermore, action research cycles are executed to develop the social enterprise business model. Based on the conceptual framework and empirical evidence, the sustainable social enterprise business model theory was formulated. Collectively, conceptual framework, action research study, and theoretical model provide the following theoretical and empirical contributions:

To begin with, the inquiry provides an important contribution in the form of a conceptual framework. It identifies the business model factors, innovation elements, and the interaction between them through the business model change. The key resources, revenue, and cost factors of the business model identified and introduced in this conceptual framework contribute to a better understanding of the activities of the social enterprise and how it influences the sustainability of the social enterprise. Furthermore, the conceptual model introduced a business model innovation framework. Specifically, it proposed the applicability of innovation elements of social finance, dual pricing, and BOP segment as factors of the BMI framework underpinning the conceptual framework. As such, the conceptual framework provided new insights into the potential mechanism through which a social enterprise business model achieves sustainability.

Moving on, the action research study provided an empirical contribution to the social enterprise literature by developing a social enterprise business model and highlighted evidence regarding the social mission along with financial sustainability related to social enterprise. The findings of this study represent an empirical contribution by identifying the financial sustainability of the social enterprise through a dual price mechanism. The financial statement from the social enterprise has offered an empirical contribution and reveals insights about the perpetuity attribute of cash waqf investment in equity capital funding of the social enterprise. Finally, the phenomenological inquiry also provided an important theoretical contribution in the form of new theoretical model with four constructs and propositions in an inductive theory-building process. The study, therefore, built a new theory explaining the financial sustainability of social enterprise through social investment in equity capital funding from the perspective of social investors.

Practical implications of the study

In this study, there are several valuable practical implications for social entrepreneurs in India that seek to obtain financial sustainability of healthcare social enterprise and provide affordable healthcare services in India. The study also has implications for social investors to define decision-making criteria for their cash waqf investments. The study improves the understanding of concepts related to the sustainable business model and the Islamic concept of cash waqf investment that is often lacking among social entrepreneurs and social investors since many of them have limited knowledge of cash waqf investment. This eliminates the ambiguity that exists with the concepts and constructs, which makes it difficult to use cash waqf investment in equity capital funding of social enterprise.

Firstly, social entrepreneurs should identify the social mission of the organization that could solve the healthcare problems of the society and ensure that underprivileged communities are included and offered affordable and continuous healthcare services. In this way, the objective of cash waqf for a religious cause that benefits human beings and promotes social welfare would be met. In turn, this would inform the investing criteria of social investors, thus ensuring that investments made in the equity capital funding of social enterprise correspond to the objectives of cash waqf and subsequently attract investment in social enterprise. A thorough understanding of cash waqf and its features among social entrepreneurs would facilitate bringing equity capital funding in the form of cash waqf to social enterprises.

Secondly, the social entrepreneur in an organization can use the SSEBM theoretical model conceptualized and developed in this study as a guideline to develop a sustainable business model of social enterprise, such that the organization is financially sustainable while working on achieving the social mission of the organization. Such financial sustainability, particularly with the integration of innovative financing, would justify the perpetuity of cash waqf, enhancing the decision and confidence of social investors and helping them to invest as cash waqf in equity capital funding of social enterprise. The cash waqf investments will ensure that the business model is successful in achieving the necessary financial sustainability of the social enterprise.

Thirdly, social investors should consider a sustainable social enterprise business model to benefit society by investing their social investment in equity capital funding that can be considered as cash waqf. In this way, social investors would reform the culture of social entrepreneurship and infuse noble practices in the utilization of cash waqf that would not only make healthcare social enterprises achieve financial sustainability but also help them to achieve the social mission by providing affordable healthcare services in India. Social investors must also review the performance of their cash waqf investments in their investee organizations on a regular basis in order to not only evaluate the financial sustainability of social enterprises but also to take corrective action and make necessary suggestions to ensure that social enterprises produce the desired financial and social results.

Limitations of the study

Even though there are several valuable practical implications for this study, there are certain limitations as well. To begin with, the study is conducted within a single social enterprise, which is a Mumbai-based social enterprise in healthcare settings. The social enterprise is a provider of healthcare services addressing the societal needs related to healthcare. Other sorts of social enterprises or a similar social enterprise in a different region, may have a different manner of doing business, resulting in different sustainable healthcare social enterprise business models. Furthermore, the idea of a sustainable social enterprise business model with the integration of innovative financing through the business model change process is just one example. There may be other ways to develop a sustainable business model of social enterprises. Thus, further research in other regions, types of social enterprise, and processes are needed to enhance the data collected from this study.

Adding on, the action research was conducted based on the conceptual model and used to evaluate the financial sustainability of the social enterprise. However, the model developed in the conceptual framework has little predictive value. While the conceptual framework established in this study was linked to the realized contribution of sustainable social enterprise business model to offering financial sustainability from cash waqf investments in equity capital funding, there was no guarantee that social enterprises using the framework would reap the advantages because the model had not been tested rigorously. Hence, further research is needed to develop this model into a reliable and widely used conceptual framework.

To move further, the action research was conducted only for three months and demonstrated the financial sustainability to the social enterprise but did not get enough time to test the model in case of loss incurred by the self-paying patients of the social enterprise. There are many changes and adaptations in business scenarios, and the three months' time may not be sufficient to witness the complete life cycle of the business from the start until stability of the business. Therefore, in order to improve its applicability, more action research cycles are needed to build the model for each scenario of business separately.

Lastly, due to the small number of participants, it was difficult to generalize the findings. Although the phenomenological study had a sufficient number of participants, as discussed previously, and the participants came from a variety of industries, there were no indications that all investment sectors had been covered or that the unique characteristics of a specific sector had been taken into account. Furthermore, the findings of this study were based on the perspectives of participants who have worked as social investors or have had the experience of social investment. Other stakeholders such as social entrepreneurs and patients, on the other hand, were not interviewed for this study. As a result, more research is needed to incorporate the perspectives of all stakeholders.

Suggestions for future research

The significance of the research was not only to gain a deeper understanding of something that we want to know more about, it also serves as a way of recognizing everything we are still yet to be aware of. Due to the complicated nature of human beings, social science, including management research often feels daunting. However, it is a process of building understanding a little at a time. On top of that, due to the aforementioned limitations it offers, the author realized that there is no perfect research. Therefore, this book offers certain valuable suggestions for future research. Although this research offered both academic and professional contributions related to the business model and social enterprises by using an empirical study, there are a number of areas for further study. As mentioned, this direction is proposed for future research, and the basis for further development of the conceptual framework for the applicability of the sustainable social enterprise business model is laid out. The direction and foundation of this research study could be of help to other researchers in the field of social enterprise and sustainable business models. The recommendations for further research are as follows:

Firstly, given the potential of sustainable social enterprise business model developed in the conceptual study to provide financial sustainability to social enterprises, as the literature and awareness on two areas of "business model" and "shariah-based endowment investment" together is still early in its growth, work on the subject is further required. Possible directions for further study could include longitudinal analysis following a cash waqf investment throughout the components of the business model to obtain more information about the ongoing dynamics of financial sustainability. In addition, exploring why some business models fail while others succeed is needed to develop a better understanding of how a sustainable social enterprise business model can be effectively applied in each component of the business model of social enterprise.

Secondly, the conceptual framework of this research was developed based on the integration of financing innovation in the business model innovation through the business model change process to attain the financial sustainability of the social enterprise. Although, SSEBM conceptual framework can be applied in any social enterprise focusing on sustainable and continuous support to the welfare of the society. However, the SSEBM conceptual framework was restricted to the healthcare domain. Thus, further study is recommended in order to extend the conceptual framework by expanding and improving its structures, as well as exposing new features in the different domains such as education, children and women welfare, etc. In this regard, the relevant frameworks of other researchers in related domains, particularly sustainable social enterprise, business model innovation, and business model change, could also be helpful.

Thirdly, a comparative analysis of cash waqf investment in social enterprises in different countries could be interesting to study if there are variations in the motivations, dynamics, and characteristics of the cash waqf investments.

Fourthly, the action research conducted to develop the sustainable social enterprise business model focused on an empirical study of organizational change regarding the financial sustainability realized from the cash waqf investment. However, the study did not consider the organizational changes that can occur after a business loss. As a result, future research should look into the occurrence of business loss and a lack of financial sustainability of social enterprise affecting the decision-making process of social investors. The influence of business loss may have an impact on the financial sustainability of the social enterprise, which may, in turn, affect the decision-making process of social investors. Future studies could discover whether social investors retain their cash waqf investments, or infuse more investment, in order to remedy the business loss and to support the sustainable business model of the social enterprise.

Finally, innovation in the business model requires change, which includes learning. Further research should explore how, as opposed to an individual perspective, social enterprises learn from an organizational perspective. This can benefit social enterprises that are larger in size and are invested by groups of social investors and operated by a team of social entrepreneurs rather than by a small number of social investors and social entrepreneurs.

BIBLIOGRAPHY

Introduction

[1] Freer Spreckley (1981). Social Audit – A Management Tool for Co-operative Working. Beechwood College.

[2] Borzaga, C., & Defourny, J. (Eds.). (2001). The Emergence of Social Enterprise. London: Routledge.

Chapter 1

[1] Russian National Research Medical University (2023). N.I. Pirogova https://studfile.net/preview/3568696/

[2] Newborn Mortality (under 5 years) [https://www.who.int/news-room/fact-sheets/detail/levels-and-trends-in-child-mortality-report-2021].

Chapter 2

[1] Liaropoulos, L. and Goranitis, I. (2015) Health Care Financing and the Sustainability of Health Systems. International Journal for Equity in Health, 14, 80.

[2] OECD (2003), OECD Health data. Available online at http://www.oecd.org/document/39/0,234,en_2649_201185_2789735_I_I_I_,00.html

[3] ILO (2021). World Employment and Social Outlook: The role of digital labour platforms in transforming the world of work. (WESO) https://www.ilo.org/wcmsp5/groups/public/—dgreports/—dcomm/—publ/documents/publication/wcms_771749.pdf.

[4] Evans R. (1981). Incomplete Vertical Integration: The Distinctive Structure of the Health-Care Industry. Health, economics, and health economics, J. J. Van der Graag, ed., Amsterdam.

[5] WHO (2003). Guide to Producing National Health Accounts. Geneva.

[6] WHO (2007). Strengthening Health Systems to Improve Health Outcomes. Geneva.

[7] Gerard Anderson and Peter S. Hussey. (2001). Trends in Expenditures, Access, and Outcomes among Industrialized Countries. In Global Health Care Markets, edited by Walter Wieners, 24–40. San Francisco, CA: Jossey-Bass.

[8] Burton Weisbrod. (1991). The Healthcare Quadrilemma: An Essay on Technological Change, Insurance, Quality of Care, and Cost Containment. Journal of Economic Literature 29(2):523–552.

[9] GIIN (2023). Impact Investing. https://thegiin.org/impact-investing/need-to-know/#what-is-impact-investing.

Chapter 3

[1] UNICEF (2023). Child poverty. Available at: https://www.unicef.org/social-policy/child-poverty.

[2] Cizakca, M. (2004). Cash waqf as alternative to NBFIs bank, paper presented at the International Seminar on Nonbank Financial Institutions: Islamic Alternatives, 1-3 March, Kuala Lumpur.

[3] Tohirin, A. (2010). The cash waqf for empowering the small businesses. paper presented at the 7th International Conference on the Tawhidi Epistemology: Zakat and Waqf Economy, Bangi.

[4] Duasa, J. and Thaker, M.A.M.T. (2016). A cash waqf investment model: an alternative model for financing micro-enterprises in Malaysia. Journal of Islamic Monetary Economics and Finance, Vol. 1 No. 2, pp. 161-188.

[5] Zakaria, A. A. M., Samad, R. R. A., & Shafii, Z. (2013). Venture Philanthropy Waqf Model: A Conceptual Study. Jurnal Pengurusan, 38, 119–125.

[6] Mohsin, M. I. A. (2013). Financing through cash-waqf: a revitalization to finance different needs. International Journal of Islamic and Middle Eastern Finance and Management, 6(4), 304-321.

Chapter 4

[1] Handford P. (2005). Guide to Financing for Social Enterprise, Western Economic Diversification Canada.

[2] Van Gils P. (2005). Fundamentals of CED Finance. Making Waves 11.

[3] Benjamin R. (2021). Impact Investing: A Theory of Financing Social Enterprises. Harvard Business School Entrepreneurial Management Working Paper No. 20-078, Available at SSRN: https://ssrn.com/abstract=3535731.

[4] Pastor, Lubos, Robert F. Stambaugh, and Lucian A. Taylor (2020). Sustainable investing in equilibrium. Journal of Financial Economics Forthcoming.

[5] Chowdhry, Bhagwan, Shaun William Davies, and Brian Waters. (2019). Investing for impact. Review of Financial Studies.

[6] EVPA Knowledge Centre (2018) A Practical Guide to Venture Philanthropy and Social Impact Investment. 4th Edition. EVPA.

[7] Osterwalder, A., & Pigneur, Y. (2010). Business Model Generation: A Handbook for Visionaries, Game Changers, and Challengers. Hoboken: Wiley.

[8] Kindström, D., & Kowalkowski, C. (2014). Service innovation in product-centric firms: a multidimensional business model perspective. Journal of Business & Industrial Marketing, 29(2).

[9] Abramson, A. & Billings, K. (2019). Challenges Facing Social Enterprises in the United States. Nonprofit Policy Forum, 10(2), 20180046. https://doi.org/10.1515/npf-2018-0046.

[10] Rizzello, A., Kabli, A. (2020). Social Finance and Sustainable Development Goals: A Literature Synthesis, Current Approaches and Research Agenda. ACRN Journal of Finance and Risk Perspectives. 9. 120-136.

[11] Jablonski, A. (2016). Scalability of Sustainable Business Models in Hybrid Organizations. Sustainability. 8.

[12] Mohd. Zain, Nor Razinah and Nur Fauziah, Najim and Zakariyah, Habeebullah and Mohd Noor, Azman. (2021). Financing social enterprises through cash waqf: an innovation of business model. In: Handbook of research on Islamic social finance and economic recovery after a global health crisis. IGI Publisher, USA, ISBN 9781799868118.

Chapter 5

[1] Castellas, E.I.-P., Ormiston, J. and Findlay, S. (2018). Financing social entrepreneurship: The role of impact investment in shaping social enterprise in Australia, Social Enterprise Journal, Vol. 14 No. 2, pp. 130-155.

[2] Biancone, Paolo Pietro & Radwan, Maha. (2019). Social Finance and Financing Social Enterprises: An Islamic Finance Prospective. European Journal of Islamic Finance.

[3] Mohd. Zain, Nor Razinah and Nur Fauziah, Najim and Zakariyah, Habeebullah and Mohd Noor, Azman. (2021). Financing social enterprises through cash waqf: an innovation of business model. In: Handbook of research on Islamic social finance and economic recovery after a global health crisis. IGI Publisher, USA, pp. 214-227. ISBN 9781799868118.

Chapter 6

[1] Global Reporting Initiative – GRI. (2013). G4 sustainability reporting guidelines: reporting principles and standard disclosures. Amsterdam.

[2] Bagnoli, L., & Megali, C. (2011). Measuring performance in social enterprises. Nonprofit and Voluntary Sector Quarterly, 40(1), 149–165.

[3] Kandaiya, M. (2020). Social enterprise and financial sustainability in South Asia: A grounded theory. Third Sector Review, 26(1), 35–65.

[4] Schoormann, Thorsten., Behrens, Dennis., Kolek, Erik., and Knackstedt, Ralf. (2016). Sustainability in business models - A literature-review-based design-science-oriented research agenad. Research Papers. 134.

[5] Lee, E. (2015). Examining the sustainability of social enterprise in contemporary Korea.

[6] Zhaoqiang, Y. (2022). Theoretical Framework of Business Model Innovation Exploration for Sustainable Development. In: Kumar, V., Leng, J., Akberdina, V., Kuzmin, E. (eds) Digital Transformation in Industry. Lecture Notes in Information Systems and Organisation, vol 54. Springer, Cham. https://doi.org/10.1007/978-3-030-94617-3_20.

[7] Clinton, L., & Whisnant, R. (2014). Model Behavior—20 Business Model Innovations for Sustainability. Sustainability Report.

[8] Stubbs, W. & Cocklin, C. (2008). Conceptualizing a Sustainability Business Model. Organization and Environment, 21(2), pp.103–127.

[9] Birkin, F. et al., (2007). New Sustainable Business Models in China. Business Strategy and the Environment, 18(1), pp.64–77.

[10] Florian, F.L. (2010). Towards a Conceptual Framework of Business Models for Sustainability. In Knowledge Collaboration & Learning for Sustainable Innovation.

[11] Cavalcante, S., Kesting, P., & Ulhøi, J. (2011). Business model dynamics and innovation: (Re)establishing the missing linkages. Management Decision, 49(8), 1327-1342.

[12] Grachev, A.V. (2010). Financial stability of an enterprise: criteria and methods of estimation in market economy. Moscow, DiS.

[13] Doncova, L.V. & Nikiforova, N.A. (2015). Financial Statement Analysis. Moscow, DiS.

[14] Giesen, E., Berman, S.J., Bell, R. and Blitz, A. (2007). Three ways to successfully innovate your business model, Strategy and Leadership, 35(6).

ABOUT THE AUTHOR

Dr. Mohammed Aslam Khan is the Chairman and Managing Director of Octaware Technologies Limited. He is an experienced technologist, result-oriented business leader, and visionary social entrepreneur with a proven track record of leading strategy development and execution to deliver rapid growth and scalable sustained profitability.

Driven by his passion for entrepreneurship, he is a staunch believer in the idea of economic and social development through entrepreneurship. Dr. Aslam has carried this belief into his vision for Octaware and its group companies – "To serve, add value and create growth for individuals, businesses and social entities".

Prior to the inception of Octaware in 2005, he was the Director of AskMe Corporation– Seattle, where he established AskMe's wholly-owned subsidiary in India, which was later acquired by RealCom Software Inc, Japan. Before AskMe, he worked as a lead developer on the Windows2000 family of products at Microsoft Corporation, Redmond, USA. Earlier, he worked at Citibank N.A., Japan, developing software for financial trading platforms.

A self-taught serial entrepreneur and socially responsible investor, he has strived towards establishing numerous healthcare businesses, including a multi-specialty hospital and rehabilitation center in India. His philanthropic contributions are channeled through RIDA Foundation - a BSE-Sammaan CSR Exchange listed Charitable Trust he has created, along with a group of academic, medical, and corporate professionals, to improve the quality of life of the needy through meaningful education and medical assistance. He is also leading an initiative to promote innovation and entrepreneurship through a business incubator and accelerator facility for start-ups. He was instrumental in conceptualizing and building a Quality Assurance Lab for the National Association of Blind (Employment &Training) to generate employment opportunities for the Visually Challenged in the I.T. industry.

Dr. Aslam holds a Bachelor of Engineering degree from the University of Mumbai, a Master of Research from Lancaster University, U.K., a Ph.D. in Business Management from the

University of Finance, Business and Entrepreneurship, Sofia, and completed his Postdoctoral Fellowship at Markfield Institute of Higher Education, Leicestershire, U.K. He has completed a yearlong SEED Transformation Program at Stanford University Graduate School of Business and a One-Year Advanced Management Program at the Indian Institute of Management, Calcutta. Dr. Aslam has secured executive education at Harvard Business School, MIT's Sloan School of Management, Said Business School of Oxford University, and Judge Business School of Cambridge University.

He is a member of the Executive Committee of the Electronics and Computer Software Export Promotion Council (ESC), sponsored by the Government of India, and convenor of the Maharashtra chapter. He has been the leader of a multi-sectoral business delegation accompanying the Hon. President of India and a member of a high-powered business delegation led by the Hon. Prime Minister of India.

Dr. Aslam Khan's brainchild, Octaware Technologies Limited, got listed on the BSE –SME platform in April 2017. Transpact Enterprises Limited made a landmark beginning by becoming the first start-up listed on the BSE Start-up platform in September 2019. The listing of Transpact at BSE made the third listing in a row for three consecutive years, which has set a record entry in the London World Book of Records

www.ingramcontent.com/pod-product-compliance
Lightning Source LLC
Chambersburg PA
CBHW032359040426
42451CB00006B/62